HOW TO START YOUR OWN KENNEL OPERATION

BusinessBookstore.com

Copyright 2004-2024 by BusinessBookstore.com, LLC

All rights reserved. No part of this book may be reproduced or transmitted in any form or by any means, electronic or mechanical, including photocopying, recording, or by any information storage and retrieval system, without permission in writing from the publisher.

Reproduction or translation of any part of this work beyond that permitted by Section 107 or 108 of the 1976 United States Copyright Act without the permission of the copyright owner is unlawful. Requests for permission or further information should be addressed to the Permissions Department, BusinessBookstore.com

Third-Party Materials and Linked Materials - The publisher is not responsible for the content of those "third-party" materials which are not directly related to the publisher, and not under its control or auspices. Further, the publisher makes no representations regarding the content, products, services, advertising, or other materials available from "third-party" materials and is not responsible for the legality, decency, copyright compliance, or accuracy of information provided by those individuals/companies which have paid to be linked to this material. Additionally, the publisher will not be held liable for damage or loss (caused or alleged to be caused) in connection with the use of a "third party" material. Please be advised that when you use affiliated services or third-party materials, you may be subject to additional terms and conditions. As with a multitude of other web materials, we ask that you exercise due diligence in browsing any "outside" vendor page.

Trademark Notice - The words contained in this text which are believed to be trademarked, service marked, or otherwise to hold proprietary rights have been designated as such by use of initial capitalization. No attempt has been made to designate as trademarked or service marked any personal computer words or terms in which proprietary rights might exist. Inclusion, exclusion, or definition of a word or term is not intended to affect, or to express judgment upon, the validity of legal status of any proprietary right which may be claimed for a specific word or term.

For information regarding permission(s), write to:

BusinessBookstore.com, LLC
PO Box 270735
Flower Mound, TX 75028
copyright@businessbookstore.com

About BusinessBookstore.com

Since 2002, BusinessBookstore.com has been dedicated to helping entrepreneurs turn their dreams into reality. With over 120,000 customers served, our mission is to empower small businesses by offering practical guidance and resources. Whether you're starting a new business, seeking a second income, or aiming to boost your existing business's profitability, we provide the tools and expertise you need.

Founded by lifelong entrepreneur **Terry Allan "Blake"**, BusinessBookstore.com leverages decades of hands-on business experience. Blake's entrepreneurial journey began at 19, and he has successfully built, grown, and sold multiple businesses since then. His passion for entrepreneurship and helping others led to the creation of BusinessBookstore.com, where he shares valuable insights through comprehensive books and resources.

Hunter Allan Blake joined his father in 2020, bringing his creative talents as the Editor and Illustrator. His skills ensure our content is visually engaging and easy to understand, enhancing the overall experience for our readers.

BusinessBookstore.com specialize in high-quality books and business plans available in digital formats and hard copy. Each resource is designed to simplify the business process, offering step-by-step instructions and expert insights tailored to entrepreneurs at every stage.

> *Our goal is to help you avoid a life spent away from your loved ones, stuck in a job that doesn't inspire you. Each morning, we want you to feel motivated to work on your dreams, not someone else's. We're committed to guiding you with easy-to-follow steps through your journey. Let's make your dreams a reality together, from one entrepreneur to another.*

© 2024 BusinessBookstore.com

Go to: www.businessbookstore.com/start

Available Resources

- Blank Templates
- Checklists
- Blog Articles
- Special Offers
- Video Tutorials
- Courses
- Links to Suppliers
- List of Franchises

Book ID: B220-7318

INTRODUCTION

Welcome to 'How to Start Your Own Kennel' - the ultimate guide for aspiring small business owners looking to enter the lucrative world of pet care. Whether you're a seasoned animal lover or a budding entrepreneur, this workbook will provide you with the essential tools, strategies, and resources needed to successfully start and grow your very own kennel.

According to the American Pet Products Association, the pet industry is booming, with Americans spending over $100 billion on their furry companions in 2020 alone. With pet ownership on the rise and pet parents increasingly seeking high-quality care for their beloved pets, there has never been a better time to launch your own kennel business.

In this book, you will embark on a step-by-step journey that will take you from defining your vision and motivation to launching and growing your kennel business. Each chapter is designed as a hands-on workbook, with practical activities and checklists to guide you through the process of starting your own kennel.

Throughout this book, you will learn how to:

- Conduct thorough market research to understand industry trends and customer needs
- Identify your target audience and create customer personas to tailor your services
- Consider the option of buying a franchise and the benefits it can offer
- Analyze your competition and develop a competitive edge
- Estimate startup costs and create a budget for your kennel business
- Choose the right legal structure and register your business entity

Introduction

- Draft a comprehensive business plan to guide your operations
- Register your business name and obtain necessary licenses and permits
- Select a suitable location for your kennel and manage suppliers and inventory
- Protect your business with the right insurance policies
- Hire and train a dedicated team to deliver exceptional pet care services
- Set up the necessary technology to streamline your operations
- Prepare a launch plan and craft a branding and marketing strategy
- Establish an online presence and implement social media marketing
- Create engaging content and plan advertising and promotions
- Manage customer relationships and develop a sales strategy to drive growth

By the end of this book, you will have the knowledge and tools to turn your passion for pets into a successful kennel business. Whether you dream of opening a dog daycare, a pet boarding facility, or a grooming salon, 'How to Start Your Own Kennel' will empower you to make your dream a reality.

So, are you ready to embark on this exciting journey? Let's dive in and start building the foundation for your thriving kennel business!

Table of Contents

—— PLAN YOUR BUSINESS ——

Chapter 1 - Vision and Motivation.. 11

- Purpose: Key to Motivation & Resilience
- Goal Setting for Store Success
- Activity: Purpose Reflection
- Activity: Goal Setting Exercise

Chapter 2 - Conduct Market Research 25

- Understanding Market Trends
- Analyzing Customer Needs and Preferences
- Activity: Market Research Survey Template

Chapter 3 - Identify Your Target Audience 39

- Creating Customer Personas
- Conducting Audience Demographic Analysis
- Activity: Target Audience Persona Template

Chapter 4 - Consider Buying a Franchise 51

- Exploring Franchise Opportunities
- Benefits and Challenges of Franchising
- Activity: Franchise Evaluation Checklist

© 2024 BusinessBookstore.com

Table of Contents

Chapter 5 - Analyze Your Competition 61

- Identifying Direct and Indirect Competitors
- SWOT Analysis of Competitors
- Activity: Competitor Analysis Worksheet

Chapter 6 - Create Your Financial Plan 71

- Estimating Startup Costs
- Projecting Revenue and Expenses
- Activity: Startup Budget Template

Chapter 7 - Choose Your Legal Structure 81

- Understanding Different Legal Structures
- Registering Your Business Entity
- Activity: Legal Structure Comparison Checklist

Chapter 8 - Draft Your Business Plan 91

- Executive Summary and Company Description
- Market Analysis and Marketing Strategy
- Activity: Business Plan Outline Template

Table of Contents

START YOUR BUSINESS

Chapter 9 - Register Your Business Name 107
- Checking Name Availability and Reserving Domain
- Filing Legal Documentation
- Activity: Business Name Availability Check Form

Chapter 10 - Obtain Necessary Licenses & Permits..................115
- Researching Local Regulations and Requirements
- Applying for Licenses and Permits
- Activity: Licenses and Permits Checklist

Chapter 11 - Select Your Business Location................................123
- Assessing Location Needs and Preferences
- Site Visits and Lease Negotiation
- Activity: Location Evaluation Checklist

Chapter 12 - Manage Suppliers and Inventory 133
- Sourcing Suppliers and Negotiating Contracts
- Establishing Inventory Management Systems
- Activity: Supplier Evaluation Form

Chapter 13 - Protect Your Business with Insurance 145
- Understanding Business Insurance Needs
- Choosing the Right Insurance Policies
- Activity: Business Insurance Checklist

© 2024 BusinessBookstore.com

Table of Contents

Chapter 14 - Hire and Train Your Team 153

- Identifying Hiring Needs and Job Roles
- Recruiting and Interviewing Candidates
- Activity: Hiring Process Checklist

Chapter 15 - Set Up Your Technology 165

- Assessing Technology Requirements
- Selecting Software and Tools
- Activity: Technology Needs Assessment

Chapter 16 - Prepare Your Launch Plan 177

- Setting Launch Goals and Objectives
- Creating Launch Timeline and Marketing Strategy
- Activity: Business Launch Checklist

PROMOTE YOUR BUSINESS

Chapter 17 - Craft Your Branding Strategy 191

- Defining Brand Identity and Values
- Creating Brand Messaging and Visuals
- Activity: Branding Strategy Workbook

Chapter 18 - Design Your Marketing Strategy.......................... 203

- Defining Target Markets and Objectives
- Developing Marketing Mix
- Activity: Marketing Plan Template

Chapter 19 - Establish Your Online Presence 213

- Building a Professional Website
- Creating Engaging Social Media Profiles
- Activity: Website Checklist

Chapter 20 - Implement Social Media Marketing................... 225

- Choosing Social Media Platforms
- Creating Content and Engagement Strategies
- Activity: Social Media Strategy Planner

Chapter 21 - Create Content for Your Business........................ 237

- Content Planning and Ideation
- Content Creation and Distribution
- Activity: Content Calendar

© 2024 BusinessBookstore.com

Table of Contents

Chapter 22 - Plan Advertising and Promotions 249
- Budgeting for Advertising Campaigns
- Selecting Advertising Channels and Methods
- Activity: Advertising Campaign Planner

Chapter 23 - Manage Customer Relationships 261
- Implementing Customer Relationship Management Systems
- Providing Excellent Customer Service
- Activity: CRM Implementation Checklist

Chapter 24 - Develop Your Sales Strategy 271
- Setting Sales Targets and Goals
- Creating Sales Processes and Pipelines
- Activity: Sales Funnel Analysis

Chapter 25 - Conclusion 281
- What's Next?
- Glossary
- Additional Resources
- Franchises

Plan Your Business

Chapter 1 - Vision and Motivation

Chapter 1

Vision and Motivation

> **Key Takeaways**
> - Purpose: Key to Motivation & Resilience
> - Goal Setting for Store Success
> - Activity: Purpose Reflection
> - Activity: Goal Setting Exercise

Welcome to Chapter 1 of 'How to Start Your Own Kennel'! In this chapter, we will delve into the importance of having a clear vision and strong motivation when starting your own business. As a small business owner, your vision will serve as the guiding light that leads you towards success, while your motivation will fuel your determination to overcome challenges and obstacles along the way.

Plan Your Business

Goal Setting for Success

Setting goals is a crucial step in turning your vision into a reality. By defining specific, measurable, achievable, relevant, and time-bound (SMART) goals, you can create a roadmap for your kennel business and track your progress towards achieving your ultimate vision. Remember, goals should be challenging yet attainable, pushing you to reach new heights while staying within reach.

Purpose: Key to Motivation & Resilience

Understanding the purpose behind your kennel business is essential for staying motivated and resilient when faced with setbacks. Your purpose is the driving force that fuels your passion, inspires your team, and connects you with your target audience on a deeper level. By aligning your actions with your purpose, you can stay focused on your mission and weather any storm that comes your way.

Chapter 1 - Vision and Motivation

Purpose: Key to Motivation & Resilience

Having a clear sense of purpose is essential when starting your own kennel. Your purpose is the driving force behind your business and will keep you motivated and resilient during challenging times. It is what gives your work meaning and direction, helping you stay focused on your goals and overcome obstacles along the way.

To define your purpose, start by asking yourself why you want to start a kennel in the first place. Is it because you have a passion for dogs and want to provide them with a safe and loving environment? Or maybe you want to offer a unique service that is missing in your community? Whatever your reasons may be, it's important to articulate them clearly and concisely.

Once you have identified your purpose, write it down and keep it somewhere visible. This will serve as a constant reminder of why you are embarking on this journey and will help you stay motivated when faced with challenges. Additionally, share your purpose with your team members, if you have any, so that everyone is aligned and working towards the same goal.

Remember, your purpose can evolve over time as your business grows and changes. It's important to revisit and reassess your purpose regularly to ensure that it still resonates with you and reflects the values of your kennel. By staying true to your purpose, you will not only stay motivated and resilient but also attract like-minded customers and employees who share your vision.

Here are some tips to help you define and maintain your purpose:

- **Reflect on your values:** Consider what values are important to you and how they align with your business goals. Your purpose should be a reflection of your core beliefs and principles.

- **Set meaningful goals:** Your purpose should inspire you to set ambitious yet achievable goals for your kennel. These goals will give you a sense of direction and progress as you work towards fulfilling your purpose.

- **Stay flexible:** While it's important to have a clear purpose, it's also important to remain flexible and open to new opportunities. Your purpose should guide you, not limit you, so be willing to adapt and pivot as needed.

- **Seek feedback:** Share your purpose with trusted friends, family members, or mentors and ask for their feedback. They may offer valuable insights and suggestions that can help you refine your purpose and make it more impactful.

- **Celebrate milestones:** As you make progress towards fulfilling your purpose, take the time to celebrate your achievements. Recognizing and acknowledging your hard work will keep you motivated and energized for the journey ahead.

In conclusion, having a clear sense of purpose is crucial for starting and growing a successful kennel. It will not only keep you motivated and resilient but also attract customers and employees who share your vision. Take the time to define your purpose, revisit it regularly, and stay true to it as you navigate the ups and downs of entrepreneurship. Your purpose is your North Star, guiding you towards a fulfilling and rewarding journey in the world of dog care.

Chapter 1 - Vision and Motivation

Goal Setting for Success

Setting goals is an essential step in starting your own kennel. Goals give you a clear direction and purpose, helping you stay focused and motivated as you work towards building your business. Here are some key tips for setting goals for success:

1. **Make your goals SMART:** SMART goals are Specific, Measurable, Achievable, Relevant, and Time-bound. This means that your goals should be clear, quantifiable, realistic, aligned with your vision, and have a deadline for completion. For example, instead of setting a vague goal like "increase revenue," a SMART goal would be "increase monthly revenue by 20% within the next six months."

2. **Prioritize your goals:** It's important to prioritize your goals based on their importance and urgency. Identify which goals will have the most significant impact on your kennel's success and focus on those first. You can use a prioritization matrix or a simple list to rank your goals accordingly.

3. **Break down your goals:** Breaking down your goals into smaller, manageable tasks can make them less overwhelming and more achievable. Create a step-by-step plan for each goal, outlining the specific actions you need to take to reach it. This will help you track your progress and stay on course.

4. **Set both short-term and long-term goals:** Short-term goals are essential for immediate progress and motivation, while long-term goals provide a bigger picture of where you want your kennel to be in the future. Balance your goals by setting a mix of short-term milestones and long-term objectives to keep your momentum going.

5. **Review and adjust your goals regularly:** Goals are not set in stone, and it's okay to revise them as needed. Regularly review your progress towards your goals and make adjustments if necessary. Celebrate your achievements, learn from setbacks, and adapt your goals to stay on track towards success.

Remember, goal setting is a dynamic process that requires ongoing commitment and effort. By setting clear, achievable goals for your kennel, you can create a roadmap for success and stay motivated as you work towards building your business.

Chapter 1 - Vision and Motivation

Visit **www.BusinessBookstore.com/start** to download blank forms, etc.

Activity: Purpose Reflection

In this activity, you'll have the opportunity to reflect on the deeper purpose driving your entrepreneurial venture. Take some time to consider why you started your own business and the impact you hope to make in the world through your business. After reflecting on these questions, jot down your thoughts and insights in the space provided below.

Instructions:

1. Find a quiet and comfortable space where you can reflect without distractions.

2. Take a few deep breaths to center yourself and clear your mind.

3. Reflect on the following questions:

   - What inspired you to start your own business?
   - What values and principles do you want your business to embody?
   - How do you envision your business making a positive impact in the world?
   - What legacy do you hope to leave through your entrepreneurial journey?

4. Write down your responses in the space provided below.

_____

_____

_____

_____

© 2024 BusinessBookstore.com

Plan Your Business

5. Once you've completed your reflection, take a moment to review your answers and consider how they align with your vision for your business.

Purpose Reflection:

1. What inspired you to start your own business?

2. What values and principles do you want your business to embody?

3. How do you envision your business making a positive impact in the world?

4. What legacy do you hope to leave through your entrepreneurial journey?

5. Additional Notes or Insights:

_____

_____

_____

Take your time to reflect deeply on these questions, and don't hesitate to revisit them periodically as your business evolves. Your sense of purpose is a powerful driver of motivation and resilience on your entrepreneurial journey, so embrace it, nurture it, and let it guide you towards success in the dynamic world of business.

Chapter 1 - Vision and Motivation

Goal Setting Exercise

Now that we've explored the importance of goal setting in Chapter 1, it's time to put theory into practice and define clear objectives for your business. Below, you'll find a goal-setting exercise designed to help you articulate your goals and create a roadmap for success. Remember to be specific, measurable, achievable, relevant, and time-bound (SMART) when setting your goals.

Business Information

- Business Name: _____
- Owners Name: _____
- Date: _____

Vision Statement

Describe the long term vision for your business

_____
_____
_____
_____

Mission Statement

State the purpose of your business and its core values.

_____
_____
_____
_____

Plan Your Business

List of Goals

Write down each goal you want to accomplish. Consider goals related to growth, revenue, community impact, etc.

☑	GOALS	PRIORITY
☐		(H) (M) (L)
☐		(H) (M) (L)
☐		(H) (M) (L)
☐		(H) (M) (L)
☐		(H) (M) (L)
☐		(H) (M) (L)
☐		(H) (M) (L)
☐		(H) (M) (L)
☐		(H) (M) (L)
☐		(H) (M) (L)
☐		(H) (M) (L)

For each goal listed, assign a priority level of High, Medium, or Low based on its importance and urgency in achieving your overall vision.

- **High Priority:** Goals that are crucial to your immediate success and long-term sustainability.

- **Medium Priority:** Goals that are important but may not require immediate attention.

- **Low Priority:** Goals that are less urgent or can be deferred to a later time.

Chapter 1 - Vision and Motivation

Goal Details

Take your high priority goal and rewrite it to include specific details and measurable outcomes. Ensure clarity in what you aim to accomplish and how success will be defined.

_____
_____
_____
_____

Key Motivations

Write down the reasons why this goal is important to you. Consider how achieving this goal aligns with your vision, values, and overall business objectives.

_____
_____
_____

Actionable Tasks

Break down the goal into actionable tasks and steps that need to be completed to achieve it. Prioritize these tasks based on their importance and sequence them in a logical order to ensure smooth progress towards achieving the goal.

By following these steps, you'll effectively structure and prioritize your goals, and develop detailed plans for achieving your high priority objectives. This systematic approach will help you stay focused, motivated, and on track towards building a successful business.

© 2024 BusinessBookstore.com

Plan Your Business

Goal Details

Take your high priority goal and rewrite it to include specific details and measurable outcomes. Ensure clarity in what you aim to accomplish and how success will be defined.

_____
_____
_____
_____

Key Motivations

Write down the reasons why this goal is important to you. Consider how achieving this goal aligns with your vision, values, and overall business objectives.

_____
_____
_____

Actionable Tasks

Break down the goal into actionable tasks and steps that need to be completed to achieve it. Prioritize these tasks based on their importance and sequence them in a logical order to ensure smooth progress towards achieving the goal.

_____
_____
_____
_____
_____
_____
_____
_____

By following these steps, you'll effectively structure and prioritize your goals, and develop detailed plans for achieving your high priority objectives. This systematic approach will help you stay focused, motivated, and on track towards building a successful business.

Chapter 1 - Vision and Motivation

Goal Details

Take your high priority goal and rewrite it to include specific details and measurable outcomes. Ensure clarity in what you aim to accomplish and how success will be defined.

_____
_____
_____
_____

Key Motivations

Write down the reasons why this goal is important to you. Consider how achieving this goal aligns with your vision, values, and overall business objectives.

_____
_____
_____

Actionable Tasks

Break down the goal into actionable tasks and steps that need to be completed to achieve it. Prioritize these tasks based on their importance and sequence them in a logical order to ensure smooth progress towards achieving the goal.

By following these steps, you'll effectively structure and prioritize your goals, and develop detailed plans for achieving your high priority objectives. This systematic approach will help you stay focused, motivated, and on track towards building a successful business.

Plan Your Business

Review and Reflect

Regularly review your goals, reflect on your progress, and make adjustments as needed.

- **Date of Review:** _____
- **Progress Summary:** _____
- **Challenges Faced:** _____
- **Adjustments Needed:** _____

Visit **www.BusinessBookstore.com/start** to download blank goal forms.

Chapter 2

Conduct Market Research

Key Takeaways

- Understanding Market Trends
- Analyzing Customer Needs and Preferences
- Activity: Market Research Survey Template

Welcome to Chapter 2 of 'How to Start Your Own Kennel'! In this chapter, we will delve into the importance of conducting market research for your new kennel business. Market research is a crucial step in understanding your target audience, identifying opportunities, and making informed decisions that will set your business up for success.

As a small business owner, you may be eager to jump right into launching your kennel, but taking the time to conduct thorough market research can make a significant difference in the long-term success of your venture. By gaining insights into market trends, customer needs, and competitor landscape, you will be better equipped to tailor your products and services to meet the demands of your target audience.

Market research is not just about collecting data; it is about gaining a deep understanding of your industry and customers. By analyzing market trends, you can identify opportunities for growth and innovation. By studying customer preferences and behaviors, you can tailor your offerings to meet their specific needs. And by evaluating your competitors, you can position your kennel uniquely in the market.

Throughout this chapter, we will provide you with practical tools and exercises to guide you through the market research process. From creating a market research survey template to conducting a competitor analysis worksheet, you will have the resources you need to gather valuable insights and make informed decisions for your kennel business.

Remember, market research is an ongoing process. As your business evolves and grows, so too should your understanding of the market. By staying attuned to changes in customer preferences, industry trends, and competitive landscape, you can adapt your strategies and offerings to remain competitive and relevant in the market.

So, grab a pen and paper, and let's dive into the world of market research! By the end of this chapter, you will have a comprehensive understanding of your target market and be well-equipped to make strategic decisions that will drive the success of your kennel business. Let's get started!

Chapter 2 - Conduct Market Research

Understanding Market Trends

Understanding market trends is essential for the success of your kennel business. By staying informed about the latest developments in the pet industry, you can identify opportunities for growth and adapt your business strategies accordingly.

One of the key market trends in the pet industry is the increasing humanization of pets. Pet owners are treating their furry companions as members of the family, which has led to a growing demand for high-quality pet products and services. As a kennel owner, you can capitalize on this trend by offering premium boarding services, personalized grooming packages, and other luxury amenities for pets.

Another important market trend to consider is the rise of pet tech. With the advent of smart pet gadgets, such as GPS trackers, automated feeders, and pet cams, pet owners are looking for innovative ways to care for their pets. You can incorporate technology into your kennel business by offering online booking systems, live video feeds of the kennel facilities, and mobile apps for pet owners to stay connected with their pets while they are away.

Additionally, sustainability and eco-friendliness are becoming increasingly important to consumers. Pet owners are seeking out environmentally friendly products and services for their pets, such as organic pet food, biodegradable waste bags, and energy-efficient facilities. To appeal to eco-conscious pet owners, you can implement green practices in your kennel, such as using eco-friendly cleaning products, recycling waste, and reducing energy consumption.

It is also crucial to keep an eye on demographic trends in the pet industry. The millennial generation, in particular, is driving growth in the pet market as they delay having children and instead opt for furry companions. Millennials are willing to spend more on their pets and are looking for pet businesses that align with their values, such as sustainability, social responsibility, and transparency. To attract millennial pet owners to your kennel, consider offering eco-friendly services, supporting pet charities, and engaging with customers on social media platforms.

In conclusion, understanding market trends in the pet industry is vital for the success of your kennel business. By staying informed about the latest developments, such as the humanization of pets, pet tech innovations, sustainability practices, and demographic shifts, you can position your kennel as a forward-thinking and customer-centric business. Keep a close watch on market trends, adapt your strategies accordingly, and continue to innovate to meet the evolving needs of pet owners.

Analyzing Customer Needs and Preferences

Understanding your customers' needs and preferences is crucial for the success of your kennel business. By analyzing what your target market is looking for, you can tailor your services to meet their expectations and stand out from the competition.

Here are some key steps to help you analyze customer needs and preferences:

1. **Conduct Surveys and Interviews:** One of the most effective ways to understand what your customers want is by directly asking them. You can create surveys or conduct interviews to gather feedback on their preferences, expectations, and pain points. This information can help you tailor your services to better meet their needs.

2. **Analyze Customer Reviews and Feedback:** Another valuable source of information is customer reviews and feedback. Take the time to read through reviews on platforms like Google, Yelp, or social media to identify common themes or areas for improvement. By addressing any issues raised by customers, you can enhance their overall experience with your kennel.

3. **Monitor Industry Trends:** Stay informed about industry trends and developments to anticipate changing customer needs and preferences. For example, if there is a growing demand for eco-friendly pet care products, you may consider offering environmentally friendly services at your kennel to attract environmentally conscious customers.

4. **Segment Your Customer Base:** Not all customers have the same needs and preferences. By segmenting your customer base based on factors like age, income, or pet ownership status, you can better understand their unique requirements. For instance, older pet owners may prioritize comfort and security for their pets, while younger pet owners may value convenience and technology.

5. **Offer Personalized Services:** Personalization is a powerful way to cater to individual customer needs and preferences. Consider offering customizable service packages or add-on options to allow customers to tailor their experience to their specific requirements. For example, you could offer grooming services for customers with long-haired breeds or specialized playtime activities for energetic puppies.

6. **Stay Responsive and Flexible:** Customer needs and preferences can evolve over time, so it's essential to stay responsive and flexible in your approach. Be open to feedback, adapt your services based on customer input, and continuously seek ways to improve the customer experience at your kennel.

By taking the time to analyze customer needs and preferences, you can create a customer-centric business that attracts and retains loyal clients. Remember, happy customers are more likely to recommend your kennel to others and contribute to the long-term success of your business.

Chapter 2 - Conduct Market Research

Visit **www.BusinessBookstore.com/start** to download blank forms, etc.

Activity: Market Research Survey Template

Now that you've learned about the importance of conducting market research and analyzing customer needs and preferences, it's time to put your knowledge into action. Use the following Market Research Survey Template to gather valuable insights from your target audience. This survey template includes topics discussed in this and previous chapters, helping you systematically collect data to inform your business decisions.

Instructions:

1. Review each question in the survey template carefully.

2. Customize the survey to align with your business goals and target audience.

3. Distribute the survey to your target audience through email, social media, or other channels.

4. Collect and analyze the survey responses to identify trends, patterns, and actionable insights.

5. Use the insights gained from the survey to refine your business strategy, product offerings, and marketing initiatives.

© 2024 BusinessBookstore.com

Market Research Survey Template:

1. Demographic Information:

- Age: _____
- Gender: _____
- Location: _____
- Occupation: _____

2. Product/Service Usage:

- Have you used similar products/services in the past? (Yes/No)

- If yes, please specify the products/services you have used:

    _____

    _____

    _____

- What factors influenced your decision to use/not use these products/services?

    _____

    _____

    _____

3. Needs and Preferences:

- What are the primary needs or problems you seek to address when considering products/services in this category?

- What features or attributes are most important to you when choosing a product/service?

- How do you prefer to purchase or access products/services in this category? (In-store, online, mobile app, etc.)

4. Competitor Analysis:

- Are you aware of any competitors offering similar products/services? (Yes/No)

  _____

  _____

- If yes, please specify the competitors you are aware of:

  _____

  _____

- How would you compare the offerings of our business to those of our competitors?

  _____

  _____

  _____

5. Brand Perception:

- What comes to mind when you think of our brand/business?

  _____
  _____
  _____

- How would you describe the reputation or image of our brand/business?

  _____
  _____
  _____

- What factors influence your perception of our brand/business positively or negatively?

  _____
  _____
  _____

6. Marketing and Communication Channels:

- How do you prefer to receive information about products/services in this category? (Email, social media, advertisements, etc.)

_____

_____

- Have you interacted with our brand/business through any marketing or communication channels? (Yes/No)
- If yes, please specify the channels you have interacted with:

_____

_____

7. Feedback and Suggestions:

- Do you have any additional feedback or suggestions for improving our products/services or customer experience?

_____

_____

Conclusion:

Completing the Market Research Survey Template provides valuable insights into the needs, preferences, and perceptions of your target audience. Use the findings to refine your business strategy, enhance your offerings, and better meet the needs of your customers. Remember, ongoing market research is essential for staying informed about evolving consumer trends and maintaining a competitive edge in the marketplace.

Chapter 3

Identify Your Target Audience

> **Key Takeaways**
>
> - Creating Customer Personas
> - Conducting Audience Demographic Analysis
> - Activity: Target Audience Persona Template

Welcome to Chapter 3 of 'How to Start Your Own Kennel'! In this chapter, we will delve into the crucial step of identifying your target audience. Understanding who your customers are is essential for the success of your kennel business. By pinpointing your target audience, you can tailor your products and services to meet their needs and preferences, ultimately leading to increased customer satisfaction and loyalty.

As a small business owner, it is important to recognize that not every pet owner will be your ideal customer. By identifying your target audience, you can focus your marketing efforts on reaching those individuals who are most likely to benefit from your services. This targeted approach can help you maximize your resources and achieve a higher return on investment.

Throughout this chapter, we will guide you through the process of creating customer personas and conducting audience demographic analysis. By the end of this chapter, you will have a clear understanding of who your target audience is, what their needs and preferences are, and how you can effectively reach and engage with them.

Remember, identifying your target audience is not a one-time task. As your business grows and evolves, so too may your target audience. It is important to regularly revisit and refine your target audience to ensure that your marketing efforts remain relevant and effective.

By the end of this chapter, you will have the tools and knowledge necessary to confidently identify and target your ideal customers. So, let's dive in and start identifying your target audience!

Creating Customer Personas

Customer personas are fictional representations of your ideal customers based on market research and real data about your existing customers. Creating customer personas helps you better understand and target your audience, tailor your products and services to their needs, and improve your marketing strategies.

Why are customer personas important?

Customer personas provide valuable insights into the behaviors, preferences, and needs of your target audience. By creating detailed personas, you can personalize your marketing messages, product offerings, and customer interactions to better meet the needs of your customers.

How to create customer personas:

1. **Conduct Market Research:** Start by analyzing your existing customer data, conducting surveys, and studying market trends to gather information about your target audience.

2. **Identify Common Characteristics:** Look for patterns and similarities among your customers, such as demographics, interests, behaviors, and pain points.

3. **Create Persona Profiles:** Develop detailed profiles for each persona, including their name, age, occupation, goals, challenges, and preferences.

4. **Use Real Data:** Base your personas on real data and insights from your research rather than making assumptions about your audience.

5. **Include Personal Stories:** Give each persona a backstory to humanize them and make it easier to empathize with their needs and motivations.

6. **Validate and Refine:** Continuously update and refine your personas as you gather more data and insights from customer interactions and feedback.

Example of a Customer Persona:

- **Name:** Sarah Smith
- **Age:** 35
- **Occupation:** Marketing Manager
- **Goals:** Increase brand awareness for her company, improve lead generation, stay updated on industry trends
- **Challenges:** Limited budget for marketing campaigns, lack of time to research and implement new strategies
- **Preferences:** Prefers digital marketing channels, values data-driven decision-making, attends industry conferences and networking events

By creating customer personas like Sarah Smith, you can tailor your marketing efforts to resonate with her specific needs and preferences. This personalized approach can help you attract and retain customers who are more likely to engage with your business.

Chapter 3 - Identify Your Target Audience

Conducting Audience Demographic Analysis

Conducting Audience Demographic Analysis is a crucial step in starting your own kennel. By understanding the demographics of your target audience, you can tailor your products and services to better meet their needs and preferences. Here are some key steps to help you conduct a thorough demographic analysis:

1. **Define Your Target Audience:** Start by clearly defining who your target audience is. Consider factors such as age, gender, income level, location, and interests. For example, if you are targeting busy professionals who live in urban areas, your services may need to focus on convenience and accessibility.

2. **Collect Data:** Gather data on your target audience through surveys, interviews, and online research. You can also use tools like Google Analytics to track website visitors and social media insights to understand your audience's online behavior.

3. **Analyze Data:** Once you have collected data, analyze it to identify trends and patterns. Look for common characteristics among your audience, such as common interests or purchasing behaviors. This will help you tailor your marketing strategies to better reach your target audience.

4. **Create Customer Personas:** Develop customer personas based on your demographic analysis. Customer personas are fictional representations of your ideal customers, including details such as age, occupation, hobbies, and pain points. Creating personas can help you better understand and empathize with your target audience.

5. **Identify Opportunities:** Use your demographic analysis to identify opportunities for growth and expansion. For example, if you discover that there is a high demand for dog grooming services in your area, you may consider adding grooming services to your kennel offerings.

Remember that conducting audience demographic analysis is an ongoing process. As your business grows and evolves, so too will your target audience. Stay informed about changes in demographic trends and continue to gather data to ensure that your products and services remain relevant to your audience.

Chapter 3 - Identify Your Target Audience

Visit **www.BusinessBookstore.com/start** to download blank forms, etc.

Activity: Target Audience Persona Template

Now that you've gathered insights about your target audience through demographic analysis and other research methods, it's time to create detailed customer personas. Use the following Target Audience Persona Template to develop personas that represent different segments of your audience. This template will help you humanize your audience and gain a deeper understanding of their needs, motivations, and preferences.

Instructions:

1. Review each section of the persona template carefully.

2. Fill in the details based on the insights and data you've gathered about your target audience.

3. Create multiple personas to represent distinct segments within your audience, if applicable.

4. Use the personas to inform your marketing strategies, product development, and customer engagement initiatives.

© 2024 BusinessBookstore.com

Plan Your Business

Target Audience Persona Template: _____

Persona Name: _____

Demographics:

- Age: _____
- Gender: _____
- Location: _____
- Occupation: _____
- Income Level: _____
- Education Level: _____

Background:

- Brief description of the persona's background and lifestyle.

  _____
  _____
  _____

- Family status (if applicable).

  _____
  _____
  _____

Chapter 3 - Identify Your Target Audience

Goals and Objectives:

- Primary goals and objectives of the persona related to your product or service.

   _____
   _____
   _____

- Secondary goals and aspirations.

   _____
   _____
   _____

Challenges and Pain Points:

- Key challenges or pain points the persona faces in relation to your product or service.

   _____
   _____
   _____

- Common obstacles or frustrations.

   _____
   _____
   _____

Motivations and Values:

- Motivations and values that drive the persona's decision-making process.

_____

_____

_____

- What matters most to them in life and business.

_____

_____

_____

Behaviors and Preferences:

- Buying behaviors and preferences related to your product/service.

_____

_____

_____

- Preferred communication channels and media consumption habits.

_____

_____

_____

Chapter 3 - Identify Your Target Audience

- Hobbies, interests, and lifestyle preferences.

_____

_____

_____

Quotes and Insights:

- Direct quotes or insights gathered from interviews, surveys, or observations.

_____

_____

_____

- What the persona says about your product or service.

_____

_____

_____

Conclusion:

Completing the Target Audience Persona Template provides you with a deeper understanding of the diverse needs and preferences of your target audience. Use the personas to tailor your strategies and initiatives to resonate with different audience segments effectively. Remember, personas are dynamic and should be updated regularly as you gather new insights and evolve your business strategies.

Chapter 4 - Consider Buying a Franchise

Chapter 4

Consider Buying a Franchise

Key Takeaways

- Exploring Franchise Opportunities
- Benefits and Challenges of Franchising
- Activity: Franchise Evaluation Checklist

Are you a small business owner looking to expand your operations and reach a wider audience? Have you considered the benefits of buying a franchise to accelerate your growth and success? In this chapter, we will explore the world of franchising and help you understand if it is the right path for your business.

Franchising offers a unique opportunity for entrepreneurs to leverage an established brand, proven business model, and ongoing support from the franchisor. By buying a franchise, you can tap into the success of a well-known brand and benefit from their marketing efforts, operational systems, and training programs.

One of the key advantages of buying a franchise is the reduced risk compared to starting a business from scratch. Franchises have a higher success rate than independent businesses because they come with a built-in customer base and a recognized brand name. This can help you attract customers more easily and generate revenue faster.

Furthermore, buying a franchise allows you to access a network of fellow franchisees who can offer guidance, support, and best practices for running a successful business. You will be part of a community of like-minded entrepreneurs who are all working towards a common goal of growing their businesses and achieving success.

Before you consider buying a franchise, it is important to do your research and due diligence. You should evaluate the reputation of the franchisor, the financial requirements, the terms of the franchise agreement, and the support and training provided. It is crucial to choose a franchise that aligns with your values, goals, and vision for your business.

Throughout this chapter, we will guide you through the process of exploring franchise opportunities, understanding the benefits and challenges of franchising, and evaluating whether buying a franchise is the right decision for your business. By the end of this chapter, you will have the knowledge and tools to make an informed choice about whether franchising is the right path for your business.

So, if you are ready to take your business to the next level and accelerate your growth, consider buying a franchise. With the right research, planning, and mindset, franchising can be a rewarding and lucrative opportunity for small business owners like you. Let's dive into the world of franchising and explore the possibilities that await you!

Chapter 4 - Consider Buying a Franchise

Exploring Franchise Opportunities

When starting your own kennel, one option to consider is buying a franchise. Franchising can provide you with a proven business model, brand recognition, and support from the franchisor. However, it is important to thoroughly research and evaluate franchise opportunities before making a decision.

Exploring Franchise Opportunities

Before diving into the world of franchising, it is essential to understand the different types of kennel franchises available. Some franchises may focus on specific services such as dog grooming, dog training, or pet boarding, while others may offer a combination of services. Research various kennel franchises to determine which one aligns best with your goals and interests.

When exploring franchise opportunities, consider the following factors:

- **Franchise Costs:** Evaluate the initial franchise fee, ongoing royalties, and any additional costs associated with the franchise. Make sure to calculate the total investment required and determine if it fits within your budget.

- **Support and Training:** Look for franchises that offer comprehensive training programs, ongoing support, and marketing assistance. A strong franchisor will provide the tools and resources you need to succeed.

- **Brand Reputation:** Research the reputation of the franchise and its brand recognition in the market. A well-established and reputable brand can attract more customers and help you build credibility.

- **Franchise Agreement:** Review the franchise agreement carefully and seek legal advice if needed. Make sure you understand the terms and conditions of the agreement, including your rights and obligations as a franchisee.

It is also recommended to reach out to current franchisees to get firsthand insights into their experiences with the franchise. Ask about their satisfaction level, challenges they have faced, and the level of support they receive from the franchisor. This information can help you make an informed decision about whether the franchise is the right fit for you.

Keep in mind that buying a franchise is a significant investment, so take your time to research and evaluate different options before committing. Consider attending franchise expos, consulting with franchise experts, and seeking advice from other business owners to gather as much information as possible.

Remember, franchising can be a great way to start your own kennel with the support of an established brand. By exploring franchise opportunities and choosing the right one for your goals and needs, you can set yourself up for success in the pet care industry.

Chapter 4 - Consider Buying a Franchise

Benefits and Challenges of Franchising

Franchising can be an attractive option for individuals looking to start their own kennel business. It offers a proven business model, established brand recognition, and ongoing support from the franchisor. However, there are also challenges that come with franchising that potential franchisees should be aware of before making a decision.

Benefits of Franchising:

1. **Proven Business Model:** One of the biggest benefits of franchising is that you are buying into a business model that has already been proven to be successful. The franchisor has already worked out the kinks and established a system that works, which can save you a lot of time and effort in the start-up phase.

2. **Brand Recognition:** When you buy into a franchise, you are also buying into an established brand with a loyal customer base. This can give you a competitive edge in the market and help attract customers to your kennel business from day one.

3. **Ongoing Support:** Franchisors typically provide ongoing support to their franchisees, including training, marketing assistance, and operational guidance. This can be invaluable, especially for first-time business owners who may not have experience running a business.

4. **Economies of Scale:** Franchising often allows franchisees to benefit from economies of scale, such as bulk purchasing discounts and shared marketing costs. This can help lower operating costs and improve profitability.

Challenges of Franchising:

1. **Initial Investment:** Franchising typically requires a significant upfront investment, which can be a barrier for some individuals. In addition to the initial franchise fee, there are also ongoing royalties and advertising fees that must be paid to the franchisor.

2. **Lack of Control:** While franchising offers a proven business model, it also comes with restrictions on how the business is operated. Franchisees must adhere to the franchisor's rules and regulations, which can limit their ability to make independent decisions.

3. **Dependence on Franchisor:** Franchisees rely on the franchisor for ongoing support and guidance, which can be a double-edged sword. While the support can be beneficial, franchisees may feel constrained by the franchisor's decisions and policies.

4. **Brand Reputation:** As a franchisee, your business's reputation is tied to the overall brand reputation of the franchise. If the franchisor makes a misstep or faces negative publicity, it can impact your business as well.

Before deciding to franchise your kennel business, it's important to carefully weigh the benefits and challenges of franchising. Consider your financial situation, business goals, and personal preferences to determine if franchising is the right path for you. Additionally, research different franchise opportunities, speak to current franchisees, and consult with a franchise attorney to fully understand the terms and conditions of the franchise agreement.

Chapter 4 - Consider Buying a Franchise

> Visit **www.BusinessBookstore.com/start** for a current list of franchises.

Activity: Franchise Evaluation Checklist

In this activity, you'll have the opportunity to evaluate franchise opportunities for your business using our Franchise Evaluation Checklist. This checklist will guide you through the key factors to consider when assessing franchise options, helping you make informed decisions about whether franchising is the right path for your business. Follow the instructions below to complete the Franchise Evaluation Checklist:

Check the appendix for a list of franchises.

Instructions:

1. **Review Franchise Criteria**: Consider the following criteria when evaluating franchise opportunities:

   - ☐ Brand Recognition and Credibility
   - ☐ Proven Business Model
   - ☐ Initial Investment Costs
   - ☐ Ongoing Fees and Royalties
   - ☐ Support Services Provided by Franchisor
   - ☐ Territory Rights and Restrictions
   - ☐ Franchise Agreement Terms and Conditions

Plan Your Business

2. **Assess Franchise Opportunities**: Research and assess multiple franchise opportunities based on the criteria outlined above. Gather information from franchisors, franchise disclosure documents (FDDs), current franchisees, and other reliable sources.

3. **Complete Franchise Evaluation Checklist**: Use the checklist below to evaluate each franchise opportunity and determine its suitability for your movie theater business.

Franchise Evaluation Checklist:

1. **Brand Recognition and Credibility**:

   ☐ Established brand with strong market presence.

   ☐ Positive reputation and consumer trust.

   ☐ Recognizable brand identity and logo.

2. **Proven Business Model**:

   ☐ Demonstrated success and profitability.

   ☐ Clear guidelines and protocols for operations.

   ☐ Track record of franchisee satisfaction.

3. **Initial Investment Costs:**

- [ ] Initial franchise fee: $ _____

- [ ] Startup costs: (including equipment, inventory, and initial marketing). $ _____

- [ ] Additional expenses: (legal fees, training costs, etc.). $ _____

4. **Ongoing Fees and Royalties:**

- [ ] Royalty fees: of gross sales. _____ %

- [ ] Advertising fees: of gross sales. _____ %

- [ ] Other ongoing fees: per month/year. _____ %

5. **Support Services Provided by Franchisor:**

- [ ] Initial training program.

- [ ] Ongoing operational support.

- [ ] Marketing and advertising assistance.

- [ ] Technology and software support.

6. **Territory Rights and Restrictions:**

    ☐   Exclusive territory rights within defined area.

    ☐   Restrictions on opening additional locations.

    ☐   Non-compete clauses and territory protection.

7. **Franchise Agreement Terms and Conditions:**

    ☐   Length of franchise term: _____ years.

    ☐   Renewal options and conditions.

    ☐   Termination clauses and exit strategies.

Take Action:

Complete the Franchise Evaluation Checklist for each franchise opportunity you're considering for your business. Use the information gathered to compare and contrast different opportunities and assess their alignment with your business goals and objectives. As you complete the checklist, consider the following question:

Which franchise opportunity best aligns with my long-term vision and objectives for my business, and why?

Use this question as a guide to making informed decisions about franchising and selecting the right opportunity to pursue your entrepreneurial dreams.

Chapter 5

Analyze Your Competition

Key Takeaways

- Identifying Direct and Indirect Competitors
- SWOT Analysis of Competitors
- Activity: Competitor Analysis Worksheet

Welcome to Chapter 5 of 'How to Start Your Own Kennel'! Analyzing your competition is a crucial step in building a successful business. By understanding who your competitors are, what they offer, and how they operate, you can identify opportunities for differentiation and growth. This chapter will guide you through the process of conducting a thorough analysis of your competitors, so you can position your kennel for success in a competitive market.

Plan Your Business

Identifying Direct and Indirect Competitors

When analyzing your competition, it's important to identify both direct and indirect competitors. Direct competitors are businesses that offer similar products or services to yours and target the same customer segment. Indirect competitors may offer different products or services but compete for the same customer dollars. By understanding the competitive landscape, you can assess your strengths and weaknesses relative to other players in the market.

SWOT Analysis of Competitors

A SWOT analysis is a strategic planning tool that helps you identify the strengths, weaknesses, opportunities, and threats of your competitors. By conducting a SWOT analysis of your competitors, you can gain valuable insights into their market position, capabilities, and potential vulnerabilities. This analysis will inform your competitive strategy and help you identify areas where you can outperform your rivals.

Activity: Competitor Analysis Worksheet

At the end of this chapter, you will find a Competitor Analysis Worksheet to help you document your findings and insights. By completing this activity, you will have a clear understanding of your competitive landscape and be better equipped to make informed decisions about how to position your kennel for success.

Remember, competition is a natural part of business, and analyzing your competitors is not about copying or imitating them. Instead, it's about understanding the market dynamics, identifying opportunities for differentiation, and leveraging your unique strengths to stand out in a crowded marketplace. By taking the time to analyze your competition, you can develop a strategic advantage that will set your kennel apart and attract loyal customers.

Chapter 5 - Analyze Your Competition

Identifying Direct and Indirect Competitors

When starting your own kennel, it is crucial to analyze your competition to understand the market landscape and identify potential threats and opportunities. Competitors can be categorized into two main types: direct competitors and indirect competitors.

Direct Competitors:

- Direct competitors are businesses that offer similar products or services to the same target audience as your kennel. They are your most immediate competition, as they are vying for the same customers and market share.

- Examples of direct competitors for a kennel may include other local dog boarding facilities, pet hotels, or doggy daycare centers.

- When identifying direct competitors, consider factors such as pricing, services offered, location, reputation, and customer reviews. This information can help you differentiate your kennel and develop a competitive advantage.

Indirect Competitors:

- Indirect competitors are businesses that offer different products or services but serve the same or similar customer needs and preferences. While they may not be direct substitutes for your kennel, they can still impact your market positioning and customer acquisition.

- Examples of indirect competitors for a kennel may include pet grooming salons, pet stores, online pet sitting platforms, or even traditional boarding facilities for other types of pets.

- It is essential to analyze indirect competitors to understand the broader pet care market and potential trends that could affect your kennel's success. Look for opportunities to collaborate or differentiate your services to attract a wider range of customers.

When conducting a SWOT analysis of your competitors, consider their strengths, weaknesses, opportunities, and threats in relation to your kennel. This exercise can help you identify gaps in the market, areas for improvement, and potential strategies to outperform your competition.

Remember that competition is a natural part of any business environment, and it can be a driving force for innovation and growth. By understanding your direct and indirect competitors, you can position your kennel effectively in the market and create a unique value proposition that resonates with pet owners.

Chapter 5 - Analyze Your Competition

SWOT Analysis of Competitors

When starting your own kennel, it's essential to analyze your competitors to understand their strengths and weaknesses. One effective way to do this is by conducting a SWOT analysis, which stands for Strengths, Weaknesses, Opportunities, and Threats.

- **Strengths:** Identify what your competitors do well. This could include factors such as a strong online presence, a loyal customer base, or unique services they offer. By recognizing their strengths, you can learn from them and find ways to differentiate your kennel.

- **Weaknesses:** Consider areas where your competitors may be lacking. This could include poor customer service, limited marketing efforts, or outdated facilities. By identifying their weaknesses, you can capitalize on those areas and offer a better experience for your customers.

- **Opportunities:** Look for opportunities in the market that your competitors are not taking advantage of. This could include expanding your services, targeting a niche market, or partnering with local businesses. By seizing these opportunities, you can gain a competitive edge and attract more customers to your kennel.

- **Threats:** Assess potential threats that could impact your kennel's success. This could include new competitors entering the market, changing customer preferences, or economic downturns. By being aware of these threats, you can develop strategies to mitigate risks and ensure your kennel's long-term viability.

It's important to regularly review and update your SWOT analysis as the competitive landscape evolves. By understanding your competitors' strengths and weaknesses, you can position your kennel for success and stand out in the market.

Chapter 5 - Analyze Your Competition

> Visit **www.BusinessBookstore.com/start** to download blank forms, etc.

Activity: Competitor Analysis Worksheet

Now that you've learned about the importance of analyzing your competitors and conducting a SWOT analysis, it's time to put that knowledge into action. The Competitor Analysis Worksheet provided below will guide you through the process of systematically gathering and organizing information about your competitors. By completing this worksheet, you'll gain valuable insights that inform your competitive strategy and position your business for success.

Instructions:

1. **Identify Your Competitors:** List the main competitors in your industry or market segment. Consider both direct and indirect competitors that may impact your business.

2. **Gather Information:** Research each competitor and gather information about their strengths, weaknesses, opportunities, and threats. Use online resources, industry reports, and customer feedback to gather insights.

3. **Complete the Worksheet:** Fill in the details for each competitor in the appropriate sections of the worksheet. Be thorough and objective in your analysis, focusing on key factors that impact their performance and market position.

4. **Analyze the Results:** Review the completed worksheet to identify trends, patterns, and areas of opportunity or concern. Use this analysis to refine your own competitive strategy and differentiate your business in the market.

© 2024 BusinessBookstore.com

Competitor Analysis Worksheet:

Competitor Name:

_____

Strengths:

List the strengths or advantages that the competitor possesses, such as strong brand reputation, innovative products, or extensive market reach.

_____

_____

_____

Weaknesses:

Identify weaknesses or vulnerabilities that may hinder the competitor's success, such as poor customer service, limited product offerings, or financial instability.

_____

_____

_____

Chapter 5 - Analyze Your Competition

Opportunities:

Highlight potential opportunities for growth or innovation that the competitor may be capitalizing on, such as emerging market trends, new customer segments, or technological advancements.

_____

_____

_____

Threats:

Identify threats or challenges that the competitor faces, such as intense competition, regulatory changes, or economic fluctuations.

_____

_____

_____

Conclusion:

Completing the Competitor Analysis Worksheet provides you with a comprehensive understanding of your competitive landscape, enabling you to identify opportunities, mitigate risks, and refine your own competitive strategy. Use the insights gained from this analysis to position your business for success and outperform your competitors in the market.

© 2024 BusinessBookstore.com

Chapter 6

Create Your Financial Plan

> **Key Takeaways**
>
> - Estimating Startup Costs
> - Projecting Revenue and Expenses
> - Activity: Startup Budget Template

Starting your own kennel is an exciting venture that requires careful planning and consideration, especially when it comes to estimating your startup costs. As a small business owner, it's essential to have a clear understanding of the financial investment required to get your kennel up and running successfully.

Estimating your startup costs involves identifying all the expenses associated with launching your kennel, from purchasing equipment and supplies to securing a suitable location and hiring staff. By taking the time to estimate your startup costs accurately, you can ensure that you have the necessary funds in place to support your business during its initial stages.

While the thought of estimating startup costs may seem daunting, it's important to remember that this process is a valuable exercise that can help you make informed decisions about your kennel's financial needs. By breaking down your expenses and creating a budget, you can set realistic financial goals and develop a solid financial plan for your business.

In this chapter, we will guide you through the process of estimating your startup costs, providing you with the tools and resources you need to make informed financial decisions for your kennel. From calculating your one-time expenses to projecting your ongoing operational costs, we will help you develop a comprehensive understanding of the financial requirements of starting and running a successful kennel.

By the end of this chapter, you will have a clear picture of the financial investment needed to launch your kennel and the confidence to move forward with your business plans. Whether you are a first-time entrepreneur or an experienced business owner, estimating your startup costs is a crucial step in building a strong foundation for your kennel's success.

So, roll up your sleeves, grab a pen and paper, and let's get started on estimating your startup costs. With dedication, determination, and a solid financial plan, you can turn your dream of owning a kennel into a reality. Let's make it happen!

Chapter 6 - Create Your Financial Plan

Estimating Startup Costs

Estimating startup costs is a crucial step in starting your own kennel. It is important to have a clear understanding of the financial requirements involved in launching your business. By accurately estimating your startup costs, you can create a realistic budget and financial plan to ensure the success of your kennel.

There are several key components to consider when estimating your startup costs:

1. **Facility Costs:** One of the biggest expenses for a kennel business is the facility itself. Consider the cost of renting or purchasing a suitable location for your kennel. Factor in expenses such as lease payments, property taxes, utilities, and renovations to make the space suitable for housing animals.

2. **Equipment and Supplies:** You will need to purchase a variety of equipment and supplies to operate your kennel effectively. This includes items such as kennels, bedding, food and water bowls, grooming supplies, cleaning supplies, and office equipment. Research suppliers to get an idea of the costs involved in acquiring these items.

3. **Licensing and Permits:** Before you can open your kennel, you will need to obtain the necessary licenses and permits to operate legally. Research the requirements in your area and budget for any fees associated with obtaining these permits.

4. **Marketing and Advertising:** To attract customers to your kennel, you will need to invest in marketing and advertising efforts. Consider the costs of creating a website, printing promotional materials, and running online or traditional advertising campaigns to promote your business.

5. **Insurance:** Protecting your business with the right insurance policies is essential. Research the types of insurance coverage you will need for your kennel, such as liability insurance, property insurance, and animal care insurance. Get quotes from different insurance providers to estimate the costs involved.

6. **Staffing Costs:** If you plan to hire employees to help run your kennel, you will need to budget for staffing costs. Consider salaries, benefits, training expenses, and any other costs associated with hiring and retaining employees.

7. **Miscellaneous Expenses:** Don't forget to account for any other miscellaneous expenses that may arise during the startup phase of your kennel business. This could include legal fees, accounting services, software subscriptions, and unexpected costs that may come up along the way.

Once you have identified all the potential costs involved in starting your kennel, create a detailed budget that outlines each expense category and the estimated costs for each item. Be sure to research prices, get quotes from suppliers, and factor in any potential contingencies to ensure that your budget is as accurate as possible.

Remember that it's always better to overestimate your startup costs rather than underestimate them. Having a cushion in your budget will help you weather any unexpected expenses that may arise as you launch your kennel business. By carefully estimating your startup costs and creating a solid financial plan, you will be better prepared to start your own successful kennel.

Chapter 6 - Create Your Financial Plan

Projecting Revenue and Expenses

When starting your own kennel, it is crucial to have a clear understanding of your projected revenue and expenses. This will help you plan and budget effectively, ensuring the financial success of your business. In this section, we will discuss how to project revenue and expenses for your kennel.

Projected Revenue:

Projected revenue refers to the income you expect to generate from your kennel business. To estimate your revenue, you will need to consider various factors such as the services you offer, pricing strategy, and target market. Here are some steps to help you project your revenue:

1. **Identify Your Services:** Start by listing all the services you plan to offer at your kennel, such as dog boarding, grooming, training, and daycare.

2. **Set Pricing:** Determine the pricing for each service based on market research, competitor analysis, and the value you provide to customers.

3. **Estimate Demand:** Research the demand for pet services in your area and assess how many customers you can attract based on your pricing and marketing efforts.

4. **Calculate Sales Forecast:** Use your pricing and estimated demand to calculate your projected sales for each service on a monthly and annual basis.

For example, if you plan to offer dog boarding at $40 per night and estimate 20 dogs staying per month, your projected monthly revenue for boarding would be $800.

Projected Expenses:

Projected expenses are the costs you anticipate incurring to operate your kennel business. It is essential to accurately estimate your expenses to avoid financial difficulties down the line. Here are some steps to help you project your expenses:

1. **List Operating Costs:** Make a list of all the expenses you will have, including rent, utilities, insurance, supplies, payroll, and marketing.

2. **Research Costs:** Research the cost of each expense item by getting quotes from suppliers, landlords, and service providers.

3. **Factor in Seasonality:** Consider any seasonal fluctuations in expenses, such as increased heating costs in winter or higher demand for services during holidays.

4. **Calculate Total Expenses:** Add up all your projected expenses on a monthly and annual basis to determine your total operating costs.

For example, if your monthly expenses for rent, utilities, supplies, and payroll total $5,000, your projected monthly operating expenses would be $5,000.

Profit Forecast:

Once you have projected your revenue and expenses, you can calculate your profit forecast by subtracting your total expenses from your total revenue. Your profit forecast will give you an idea of how profitable your kennel business can be and help you make informed decisions about pricing, cost-cutting, and growth strategies.

Remember that projecting revenue and expenses is not an exact science, and there will always be some degree of uncertainty. It is essential to regularly review and adjust your projections based on actual performance to ensure the financial health of your kennel business.

Chapter 6 - Create Your Financial Plan

> Visit **www.BusinessBookstore.com/start** to download blank forms, etc.

Activity: Startup Budget Template

As you've learned, creating a comprehensive financial plan is essential for the success and sustainability of your business. The Startup Budget Template provided below will serve as a practical tool to help you organize and plan your startup expenses, revenue projections, and overall financial outlook.

Instructions:

1. **Fill in each section:** Use the knowledge and insights gained from previous chapters to fill in each section of the Startup Budget Template with relevant information about your business.

2. **Be detailed and realistic:** Provide detailed estimates for startup expenses and revenue projections, taking into account factors such as market research, industry trends, and business assumptions.

3. **Regularly update and review:** As your business evolves, regularly update and review your startup budget to reflect changes in expenses, revenue, and overall financial performance.

Startup Budget Template:

INITIAL EXPENSES:

Business registration and legal fees:	$ _____
Lease or rental deposit:	$ _____
Utility setup fees:	$ _____
Initial inventory purchases:	$ _____
Store signage and branding:	$ _____
Technology and POS system setup:	$ _____
Furniture and fixtures:	$ _____
Initial marketing and advertising:	$ _____
Professional services (legal, accounting, etc.):	$ _____
Miscellaneous expenses:	$ _____
TOTAL Initial Expenses:	$ _____

ONGOING MONTHLY EXPENSES:

Rent or lease payments:	$ _____
Utilities (electricity, water, internet, etc.):	$ _____
Inventory purchases and restocking:	$ _____
Employee salaries and wages:	$ _____
Marketing and advertising costs:	$ _____
Insurance (business liability, property, etc.):	$ _____
Equipment maintenance and repairs:	$ _____
Professional services (accounting, legal, etc.):	$ _____
Loan repayments (if applicable):	$ _____
Miscellaneous expenses:	$ _____
TOTAL Monthly Expenses:	$ _____

Estimated monthly sales:	$ _____

Chapter 6 - Create Your Financial Plan

FUNDING SOURCES:

Personal savings:	$ _____
Small business loan:	$ _____
Investment from partners or investors:	$ _____
Grants or government funding:	$ _____
Crowdfunding or peer-to-peer lending:	$ _____
Other sources:	$ _____
TOTAL Funding:	$ _____

Conclusion:

Completing the Startup Budget Template provides you with a clear and organized view of your business's financial outlook, enabling you to make informed decisions and navigate the financial challenges of entrepreneurship with confidence. Use this tool as a guiding framework for managing your startup finances and driving success in your business.

Chapter 7

Choose Your Legal Structure

> **Key Takeaways**
>
> - Understanding Different Legal Structures
> - Registering Your Business Entity
> - Activity: Legal Structure Comparison Checklist

Welcome to Chapter 7 of 'How to Start Your Own Kennel'! In this chapter, we will guide you through the process of choosing the legal structure for your kennel business. This is a crucial step in starting your own business, as the legal structure you choose will have a significant impact on how your business operates, how it is taxed, and how it is regulated.

As a small business owner, it is important to understand the different legal structures available to you and to choose the one that best suits your needs and goals. By selecting the right legal structure for your kennel business, you can protect your personal assets, minimize your tax liability, and ensure that your business is compliant with all relevant laws and regulations.

Throughout this chapter, we will explore the various legal structures available to small business owners, including sole proprietorships, partnerships, limited liability companies (LLCs), and corporations. We will discuss the advantages and disadvantages of each structure, as well as the legal and financial implications of choosing one over the other.

By the end of this chapter, you will have a clear understanding of the different legal structures available to you, as well as the knowledge and tools you need to choose the one that is right for your kennel business. Whether you are just starting out or looking to restructure your existing business, this chapter will provide you with the guidance and resources you need to make an informed decision.

Starting a kennel business can be a rewarding and fulfilling experience, but it is important to lay a solid foundation for your business by choosing the right legal structure. With the information and insights provided in this chapter, you will be well-equipped to make the best decision for your business and set yourself up for success in the competitive pet care industry.

So, let's dive in and explore the world of legal structures for small businesses. By the end of this chapter, you will have the knowledge and confidence to choose the legal structure that is right for your kennel business and take the next steps towards turning your dream of owning a successful pet care business into a reality.

Chapter 7 - Choose Your Legal Structure

Understanding Different Legal Structures

When starting your own kennel business, one of the key decisions you will need to make is choosing the legal structure for your business. The legal structure you choose will have implications for how your business is taxed, how much personal liability you have, and the level of formality required in your business operations.

There are several common legal structures that you can choose from when starting your kennel business. Each structure has its own advantages and disadvantages, so it's important to understand the differences between them before making a decision.

Sole Proprietorship:

A sole proprietorship is the simplest form of business structure and is owned and operated by a single individual. In a sole proprietorship, the owner is personally responsible for all aspects of the business, including debts and liabilities. This means that if the business is sued or goes into debt, the owner's personal assets could be at risk.

One of the main advantages of a sole proprietorship is that it is easy and inexpensive to set up. There is no need to file any formal paperwork with the government, although you may need to obtain any necessary licenses or permits for your kennel business.

Partnership:

A partnership is a business structure in which two or more individuals share ownership of the business. There are several types of partnerships, including general partnerships, limited partnerships, and limited liability partnerships. In a general partnership, all partners share equally in the profits and losses of the business and are personally liable for the debts and obligations of the business.

One advantage of a partnership is that it allows you to pool resources and expertise with other individuals. However, it's important to have a clear partnership agreement in place that outlines each partner's rights and responsibilities to avoid potential conflicts down the road.

Limited Liability Company (LLC):

An LLC is a hybrid legal structure that combines the flexibility and tax benefits of a partnership with the limited liability of a corporation. In an LLC, the owners (known as members) are not personally liable for the debts and obligations of the business. This means that if the business is sued or goes into debt, the members' personal assets are generally protected.

One of the main advantages of an LLC is that it provides a great deal of flexibility in terms of how the business is managed and taxed. LLCs are relatively easy to set up and maintain, making them a popular choice for small businesses like kennels.

Corporation:

A corporation is a separate legal entity that is owned by shareholders. Corporations are more complex and expensive to set up than other business structures, but they offer the most protection from personal liability. In a corporation, the shareholders are not personally liable for the debts and obligations of the business.

One advantage of a corporation is that it can raise capital by selling shares of stock. However, corporations are subject to more regulations and formalities than other business structures, such as holding regular board meetings and keeping detailed financial records.

Chapter 7 - Choose Your Legal Structure

When choosing a legal structure for your kennel business, it's important to consider factors such as personal liability, tax implications, and the level of formality you are comfortable with. Consulting with a legal or financial advisor can help you make an informed decision that is best for your specific situation.

Registering Your Business Entity

Registering your business entity is a crucial step in starting your own kennel. This process involves legally establishing your business and ensuring that it complies with all relevant laws and regulations. By registering your business entity, you will be able to operate your kennel in a legitimate and professional manner.

There are several types of legal structures that you can choose from when registering your business entity. The most common types of legal structures for small businesses include sole proprietorship, partnership, limited liability company (LLC), and corporation. Each type of legal structure has its own advantages and disadvantages, so it is important to carefully consider which one is best suited for your kennel.

1. **Sole Proprietorship:** A sole proprietorship is the simplest form of business entity and is owned and operated by one individual. This type of legal structure is easy to set up and does not require any formal registration. However, as a sole proprietor, you will be personally liable for any debts or legal obligations of the business.

2. **Partnership:** A partnership is a legal structure in which two or more individuals share ownership of the business. Partnerships can be general partnerships, limited partnerships, or limited liability partnerships. Partnerships require a partnership agreement that outlines each partner's rights and responsibilities.

3. **Limited Liability Company (LLC):** An LLC is a popular choice for small businesses because it offers the limited liability protection of a corporation with the flexibility and tax benefits of a partnership. Forming an LLC involves filing articles of organization with the state and creating an operating agreement that governs the operation of the business.

4. **Corporation:** A corporation is a separate legal entity that is owned by shareholders. Corporations offer the most protection from personal liability, but they are also subject to more regulations and formalities than other types of legal structures. To form a corporation, you will need to file articles of incorporation with the state and appoint a board of directors.

When registering your business entity, you will need to choose a unique name for your kennel that is not already in use by another business. You can search the business name database in your state to check the availability of your desired business name. Once you have chosen a name, you will need to file a "Doing Business As" (DBA) or fictitious name registration with the state.

After selecting a legal structure and business name, you will need to register your business entity with the appropriate government authorities. The registration process varies depending on the type of legal structure you choose and the state in which you are operating. In general, you will need to file the necessary paperwork and pay the required fees to officially register your business entity.

It is important to consult with a legal professional or accountant when registering your business entity to ensure that you are complying with all legal requirements and maximizing the benefits of your chosen legal structure. By taking the time to properly register your business entity, you will be laying a solid foundation for the success and growth of your kennel.

Chapter 7 - Choose Your Legal Structure

> Visit **www.BusinessBookstore.com/start** to register your business.

Activity: Legal Structure Comparison Checklist

The Legal Structure Comparison Checklist provided below will assist you in evaluating and comparing different legal structures for your business. By completing this checklist, you'll gain clarity on the advantages, disadvantages, and suitability of each structure based on your specific needs and circumstances.

Instructions:

- **Review Each Legal Structure:** Familiarize yourself with the characteristics and implications of sole proprietorships, partnerships, limited liability companies (LLCs), and corporations as discussed previously.

- **Evaluate Based on Your Business Needs:** Consider factors such as liability protection, taxation, management flexibility, and regulatory requirements when assessing each legal structure.

- **Complete the Checklist:** For each legal structure, indicate whether it aligns with your business goals and preferences by checking the corresponding boxes.

- **Consider Professional Advice:** Consult with legal and financial professionals to further assess your options and make an informed decision about the most suitable legal structure for your business.

Legal Structure Comparison Checklist:

Criteria	Sole Proprietorship	Partnership	LLC	Corporation
Liability Protection				
Taxation				
Management Flexibility				
Regulatory Requirements				
Ease of Formation				
Ownership Structure				
Continuity of Existence				
Cost of Formation and Maintenance				
Tax Reporting Requirements				

Conclusion:

Completing the Legal Structure Comparison Checklist will provide you with valuable insights into the suitability of each legal structure for your business. Use this tool as a guiding framework to make an informed decision that aligns with your business goals and aspirations.

Chapter 8

Draft Your Business Plan

> **Key Takeaways**
>
> - Executive Summary and Company Description
> - Market Analysis and Marketing Strategy
> - Activity: Business Plan Outline Template

Welcome to Chapter 8 of 'How to Start Your Own Kennel'! Drafting a business plan is a crucial step in turning your dream of owning a kennel into a reality. A well-thought-out business plan not only serves as a roadmap for your business but also helps you secure funding, attract investors, and set clear goals for your success.

In this chapter, we will guide you through the process of drafting a comprehensive business plan that outlines your kennel's mission, vision, target market, marketing strategy, financial projections, and more. By the end of this chapter, you will have a solid business plan that will serve as a blueprint for your kennel's future.

Whether you are a seasoned entrepreneur or a first-time business owner, drafting a business plan can seem like a daunting task. But fear not! We have broken down the process into manageable steps and provided you with templates and tools to simplify the process.

Remember, a business plan is not set in stone and can be adjusted as your kennel grows and evolves. It is a living document that should be revisited regularly to ensure that your business remains on track and aligned with your goals.

So, roll up your sleeves, grab a pen and paper, and let's get started on drafting your business plan for your kennel. By the end of this chapter, you will have a clear roadmap for success and a deeper understanding of your business's potential.

Get ready to unleash your creativity, passion, and entrepreneurial spirit as you dive into the exciting world of business planning. Let's turn your vision of owning a successful kennel into a reality!

Chapter 8 - Draft Your Business Plan

Executive Summary and Company Description

An executive summary is a brief overview of your business plan that highlights the key points and objectives of your kennel business. It is typically the first section of your business plan that potential investors or lenders will read, so it is important to make it clear, concise, and compelling.

When writing your executive summary, you should include the following elements:

- **Business Name and Location:** Start by introducing your kennel business and where it will be located. For example, "Pawsitively Purrfect Kennels will be a premium pet boarding facility located in the heart of downtown."

- **Mission Statement:** Define the purpose and values of your kennel business. For instance, "Our mission is to provide a safe, comfortable, and loving environment for pets while their owners are away."

- **Services Offered:** Describe the services you will offer, such as boarding, grooming, training, and daycare. Highlight what sets your kennel apart from competitors.

- **Target Market:** Identify your target audience, including demographics like age, income, and pet ownership. Explain how you will reach and attract this market.

- **Revenue Model:** Outline how your kennel will generate income, whether through boarding fees, grooming services, retail sales, or other revenue streams.

- **Financial Projections:** Provide a summary of your financial projections, including startup costs, revenue forecasts, and profit margins. This will give investors a sense of the potential return on investment.

- **Growth Strategy:** Share your plans for growth and expansion, such as adding new services, opening additional locations, or targeting new markets.

- **Team Members:** Introduce key members of your team, including their backgrounds and roles in the business. Highlight any relevant experience or expertise that will contribute to the success of your kennel.

- **Unique Selling Proposition:** Clearly define what makes your kennel unique and why pet owners should choose your services over competitors. This could be your exceptional customer service, state-of-the-art facilities, or specialized care options.

Remember to keep your executive summary concise and focused, while still conveying the passion and potential of your kennel business. It should be a compelling introduction that entices readers to learn more about your company and its offerings.

Chapter 8 - Draft Your Business Plan

Market Analysis and Marketing Strategy

Market analysis and marketing strategy are crucial components of starting your own kennel. By understanding your target market and developing a solid marketing plan, you can effectively reach and attract customers to your business.

Market Analysis:

Before you can create a successful marketing strategy, you need to conduct a thorough market analysis. This involves researching your target market, understanding their needs and preferences, and identifying key trends in the industry.

One way to conduct market analysis is by using surveys to gather data from potential customers. By asking questions about their pet ownership habits, preferences for kennel services, and willingness to pay for such services, you can gain valuable insights into your target market.

Additionally, analyzing your competitors can provide valuable information about the market landscape. Identify direct and indirect competitors in your area, assess their strengths and weaknesses, and conduct a SWOT analysis to understand how your kennel can differentiate itself in the market.

Marketing Strategy:

Once you have a clear understanding of your target market, you can begin developing a marketing strategy to promote your kennel and attract customers. Your marketing strategy should outline how you will reach your target audience, communicate your unique value proposition, and drive sales for your business.

One key element of your marketing strategy is defining your target markets and objectives. Identify specific customer segments that you want to target, such as pet owners in a certain demographic or geographic area, and set clear objectives for reaching and engaging with these customers.

Another important aspect of your marketing strategy is developing your marketing mix. This includes determining which marketing channels and tactics you will use to promote your kennel, such as online advertising, social media marketing, and local promotions. By creating a well-rounded marketing mix, you can reach customers through multiple touchpoints and increase your chances of success.

It is also essential to create a budget for your marketing activities and track the effectiveness of your campaigns. By monitoring key metrics such as customer acquisition cost, return on investment, and customer lifetime value, you can optimize your marketing efforts and ensure that you are getting the most out of your budget.

Example:

For example, if your market analysis reveals that there is a high demand for dog boarding services in your area, you can tailor your marketing strategy to highlight the convenience and quality of your kennel's boarding facilities. You could create targeted social media ads showcasing happy dogs at your kennel, offer special promotions for first-time customers, and partner with local pet stores to promote your services.

Overall, market analysis and marketing strategy are essential components of starting your own kennel. By understanding your target market, developing a solid marketing plan, and executing your strategies effectively, you can attract customers to your business and set yourself up for success in the competitive pet care industry.

Chapter 8 - Draft Your Business Plan

> Visit **www.BusinessBookstore.com/start** to download blank forms, etc.

Activity: Business Plan Outline Template

Now it's time to put all the insights and strategies you've learned into action by drafting your own business plan. Below is a comprehensive Business Plan Outline Template to guide you through the process. By filling out each section of the template, you'll create a structured roadmap for your business's success.

Instructions:

1. **Review Each Section:** Familiarize yourself with the components of the Business Plan Outline Template, including Executive Summary, Company Description, Market Analysis, Marketing Strategy, Financial Plan, and more.

2. **Fill Out Each Section:** For each section, provide detailed information about your business concept, target market, competitive landscape, marketing strategies, financial projections, and operational plans. Use the insights and strategies discussed in this chapter to inform your responses.

3. **Be Clear and Concise:** Keep your responses clear, concise, and focused on key points. Highlight the unique aspects of your business and articulate your vision, goals, and strategies effectively.

4. **Seek Feedback:** Once you've completed the template, seek feedback from mentors, advisors, or peers to ensure your business plan is thorough, coherent, and compelling.

Business Plan Outline Template:

1. **Executive Summary:**

   - Overview of your business concept, mission, and objectives.

     _____
     _____
     _____

   - Summary of key components of the business plan.

     _____
     _____
     _____

   - Highlight of your unique value proposition and competitive advantage.

     _____
     _____
     _____

2. **Company Description:**

   - History, vision, and core values of your business.

     _____
     _____
     _____

- Description of products or services offered.

  _____
  _____
  _____

- Target market segments and customer demographics.

  _____
  _____
  _____

- Competitive analysis and positioning in the market.

  _____
  _____
  _____

3. **Market Analysis:**

   - Analysis of industry trends and market dynamics.

     _____
     _____
     _____

   - Segmentation of target market and customer personas.

     _____
     _____
     _____

Plan Your Business

- Competitive landscape and SWOT analysis.

  _____
  _____
  _____

- Customer insights and needs assessment.

  _____
  _____
  _____

4. **Marketing Strategy:**

   - Value proposition and unique selling proposition (USP).

     _____
     _____
     _____

   - Selection of marketing channels and tactics.

     _____
     _____
     _____

   - Content and messaging strategy.

     _____
     _____
     _____

Chapter 8 - Draft Your Business Plan

- Marketing goals and KPIs.

   _____
   _____
   _____

5. **Financial Plan:**

   - Startup costs and funding requirements.

      _____
      _____
      _____

   - Revenue projections and sales forecasts.

      _____
      _____
      _____

   Operating expenses and cost structure.

      _____
      _____
      _____

   - Cash flow projections and break-even analysis.

      _____
      _____
      _____

Plan Your Business

6. **Operational Plan:**

   - Organizational structure and management team.

     _____
     _____
     _____

   - Production or service delivery processes.

     _____
     _____
     _____

   - Technology requirements and infrastructure.

     _____
     _____
     _____

   - Suppliers, vendors, and distribution channels.

     _____
     _____
     _____

Chapter 8 - Draft Your Business Plan

7. **Appendices:**

    - Additional documents, research findings, or supporting materials.

Conclusion:

Completing the Business Plan Outline Template will provide you with a structured framework for organizing your ideas and strategies into a comprehensive business plan. Use this template as a guiding tool to articulate your vision, set goals and create a roadmap for success. Good luck on your entrepreneurial journey!

Start Your Business

Chapter 9

Register Your Business Name

> **Key Takeaways**
> - Checking Name Availability and Reserving Domain
> - Filing Legal Documentation
> - Activity: Business Name Availability Check Form

> Visit **www.BusinessHelpStore.com** to search for your business domain.

Welcome to Chapter 9 of 'How to Start Your Own Kennel'! In this chapter, we will delve into the importance of registering your business name. Choosing the right name for your kennel is a crucial step in establishing your brand identity and building credibility with your customers. By registering your business name, you not only protect your brand from being used by others but also comply with legal requirements.

As a small business owner, it is essential to understand the process of registering your business name and the benefits it brings. This chapter will guide you through the steps involved in checking the availability of your desired business name, reserving a domain name, and filing the necessary legal documentation to secure your business name.

Registering your business name is more than just a formality, it is a strategic decision that can impact the success of your kennel. A strong and memorable business name can attract customers, differentiate your kennel from competitors, and leave a lasting impression on your target audience. It is an opportunity to showcase your creativity, professionalism, and commitment to your business.

Throughout this chapter, we will provide you with practical tips, resources, and templates to simplify the process of registering your business name. Whether you are a first-time entrepreneur or a seasoned business owner, this chapter will equip you with the knowledge and tools to navigate the legal requirements and make informed decisions about your business name.

By the end of this chapter, you will have a clear understanding of the steps involved in registering your business name, the importance of choosing a unique and memorable name, and the impact it can have on your kennel's brand identity. You will be ready to take the necessary actions to secure your business name and position your kennel for success in the competitive pet care industry.

So, let's dive into Chapter 9 and learn how to register your business name effectively. Get ready to unleash the full potential of your kennel by choosing the perfect name that reflects your passion for animals and your commitment to providing exceptional care for your furry clients!

Chapter 9 - Register Your Business Name

Checking Name Availability and Reserving Domain

Before you can officially register your business name, you need to make sure that it is available and unique. This process involves checking the availability of the name for both legal and online purposes.

Checking Legal Name Availability:

First, you need to ensure that the business name you have chosen is not already in use by another company in your state or country. This can be done by searching the business name database maintained by the relevant government agency, such as the Secretary of State's office.

Here are some steps to follow when checking legal name availability:

1. Contact the Secretary of State's office or the business registration agency in your jurisdiction.

2. Use their online search tool to look up the availability of your desired business name.

3. If the name is already taken, you will need to come up with a different name or consider adding a unique identifier to your chosen name to distinguish it from existing businesses.

Start Your Business

Reserving Domain Name:

Securing a domain name that matches your business name is crucial for establishing a strong online presence. Even if you are not ready to launch a website immediately, reserving your domain name early can prevent others from using it.

Here are some tips for reserving a domain name:

- Choose a domain name that is easy to spell, remember, and reflects your business name or industry.
- Consider using a domain extension (.com, .net, .org) that is commonly associated with business websites.
- Check the availability of your desired domain name using a domain registrar or hosting provider's search tool.
- If your first choice is not available, try variations or abbreviations of your business name to find a suitable domain name.
- Register your domain name through a reputable provider to ensure security and ownership.

By checking the availability of your business name for legal purposes and reserving a domain name for your online presence, you can protect your brand identity and avoid potential conflicts with existing businesses. Take the time to research and secure these essential elements before moving forward with registering your business.

Chapter 9 - Register Your Business Name

Filing Legal Documentation

When starting your own kennel, one of the important steps you'll need to take is filing the necessary legal documentation. This process involves registering your business entity with the appropriate government authorities and obtaining the required permits and licenses to operate legally.

Here are some key steps to consider when filing legal documentation for your kennel:

1. **Choose a Legal Structure:** Before you can file any legal documentation, you'll need to decide on the legal structure of your kennel. The most common options for small businesses like kennels are sole proprietorship, partnership, limited liability company (LLC), and corporation. Each legal structure has its own advantages and disadvantages, so it's important to research and choose the one that best suits your needs.

2. **Register Your Business Entity:** Once you've chosen a legal structure, you'll need to register your business entity with the appropriate government authorities. This typically involves filing paperwork with the state or local government, paying any required fees, and obtaining a business license. The specific requirements vary depending on your location, so be sure to check with your local government for guidance.

3. **Obtain Necessary Permits and Licenses:** In addition to registering your business entity, you'll also need to obtain any necessary permits and licenses to operate your kennel legally. These may include zoning permits, animal care permits, and health department licenses. Again, the requirements vary by location, so it's important to research and comply with all regulations.

4. **File Tax Documents:** As a business owner, you'll also need to file various tax documents with the government. This may include applying for an employer identification number (EIN), filing quarterly or annual tax returns, and paying any required taxes. It's important to keep accurate records of your income and expenses to ensure compliance with tax laws.

It's important to note that the process of filing legal documentation can be complex and time-consuming, so it's a good idea to seek professional advice from a lawyer or accountant. They can help guide you through the process and ensure that you comply with all legal requirements.

By taking the time to file the necessary legal documentation for your kennel, you can establish a solid legal foundation for your business and avoid potential problems down the road. Remember, compliance with legal requirements is essential for the long-term success of your kennel.

Chapter 9 - Register Your Business Name

> Visit **www.BusinessBookstore.com/start** to register your business.

Activity: Business Name Availability Check Form

Before finalizing your business name, it's crucial to ensure that it's available for use and doesn't infringe on existing trademarks or business entities. Use the following form to conduct a thorough check of your desired business name's availability:

Business Name Availability Check Form

1. **Proposed Business Name:**_____

2. **Business Structure:** Select the business structure you're considering: Sole Proprietorship / Partnership / Limited Liability Company (LLC) / Corporation

3. **Check State Business Registry:**

   ☐ Search the online database of your state's business registry to see if the proposed name is already registered by another business entity.

   ☐ Note any similar or identical names that may pose potential conflicts.

4. **Search U.S. Patent and Trademark Office (USPTO) Database:**

   ☐ Visit the USPTO website and conduct a trademark search to determine if the proposed name is already trademarked.

   ☐ Pay attention to any existing trademarks that may overlap with your proposed business name.

5. **Domain Name Availability:**

   ☐ Check the availability of the corresponding domain name for your business.
   ☐ Search domain registration websites to see if your desired domain name is available for purchase.

6. **Additional Considerations:**

   ☐ Consider the availability of social media handles associated with your proposed business name.
   ☐ Evaluate the overall availability and uniqueness of the name in your industry and market.

7. **Final Decision:**

   ☐ Based on the results of your research, determine if the proposed business name is available for use.
   ☐ If the name is available, proceed with registering it for your business. If not, brainstorm alternative names and repeat the availability check process.

Instructions: Complete each section of the form by performing the specified actions. Be thorough in your research to ensure that your chosen business name is available and legally sound. Once you've completed the form and confirmed the availability of your desired name, you can proceed with confidence in establishing your business identity.

Chapter 10

Obtain Necessary Business Licenses and Permits

> **Key Takeaways**
> - Researching Local Regulations and Requirements
> - Applying for Licenses and Permits
> - Activity: Licenses and Permits Checklist

Welcome to Chapter 10 of 'How to Start Your Own Kennel'! As a small business owner, it is crucial to ensure that you have all the necessary licenses and permits in place before you officially launch your kennel. This chapter will guide you through the process of researching and obtaining the required documentation to operate your business legally and smoothly.

Obtaining licenses and permits may seem like a daunting task, but it is a necessary step to protect your business and comply with local regulations. By following the steps outlined in this chapter, you will be able to navigate the licensing process with confidence and ease.

Throughout this chapter, we will discuss the importance of researching local regulations and requirements, applying for the appropriate licenses and permits, and staying compliant with ongoing obligations. By proactively addressing these legal aspects of your business, you can avoid potential fines, penalties, or even the risk of closure.

Remember, each location may have specific licensing requirements for kennels, so it is essential to thoroughly research the regulations in your area. By taking the time to understand and fulfill these obligations, you can set your kennel up for long-term success and growth.

As you work through this chapter, keep in mind that obtaining licenses and permits is not just about meeting legal requirements; it is also about building trust with your customers and demonstrating your commitment to operating a reputable and professional business. By showcasing your compliance with regulations, you can instill confidence in your clients and set yourself apart from competitors.

Whether you are a first-time business owner or a seasoned entrepreneur, this chapter will provide you with the knowledge and tools you need to navigate the licensing process effectively. By staying informed and proactive, you can ensure that your kennel is operating legally and ethically, setting a solid foundation for future growth and success.

So, let's dive into the world of licenses and permits and take the necessary steps to protect and legitimize your kennel business. By the end of this chapter, you will have a clear understanding of the licensing requirements for your kennel and be ready to take the next steps towards launching your business with confidence.

Chapter 10 - Obtain Necessary Business Licenses and Permits

Researching Local Regulations and Requirements

When starting your own kennel, it is crucial to research and understand the local regulations and requirements that govern your business. These regulations can vary depending on your location, so it is important to do thorough research to ensure that you are compliant with all laws and regulations.

Researching Local Regulations:

1. Contact your local government offices, such as the city or county clerk's office, to inquire about specific regulations that apply to kennels in your area. They can provide you with information on zoning laws, licensing requirements, and any health and safety regulations that you need to follow.

2. Check with your state's Department of Agriculture or Department of Health for any additional regulations that may apply to kennels. They may have specific guidelines on animal care, sanitation, and record-keeping that you need to adhere to.

3. Research any industry-specific regulations that may apply to kennels, such as those set by organizations like the American Kennel Club or the Humane Society. These guidelines can help you ensure that you are providing the best care for the animals in your facility.

Understanding Requirements:

1. **Zoning Laws:** Check the zoning laws in your area to make sure that you are allowed to operate a kennel on the property you have chosen. Some areas may have restrictions on the types of businesses that can operate in certain zones, so it is important to verify that your kennel is permitted.

2. **Licensing:** Most jurisdictions require kennels to obtain a business license to operate legally. The process for obtaining a license can vary, so be sure to follow the instructions provided by your local government office to apply for and receive your license.

3. **Health and Safety Regulations:** Ensure that your kennel meets all health and safety standards set by your local government. This may include requirements for sanitation, ventilation, and emergency procedures to ensure the well-being of the animals in your care.

Examples of Local Regulations:

- In some areas, kennels may be required to have a certain amount of outdoor space per animal to ensure that they have room to exercise and play.
- Some jurisdictions may require kennels to have a designated quarantine area for sick animals to prevent the spread of disease.

It is essential to thoroughly research and understand the local regulations and requirements that apply to your kennel to avoid any potential legal issues and ensure the success of your business.

Chapter 10 - Obtain Necessary Business Licenses and Permits

Applying for Licenses and Permits

When starting a kennel business, one of the most important steps you need to take is applying for the necessary licenses and permits. These legal requirements are essential to ensure that your business operates legally and complies with all regulations. Here is a step-by-step guide on how to apply for licenses and permits for your kennel:

1. **Research Local Regulations:** The first step is to research the specific licenses and permits required for operating a kennel in your area. Contact your local government office or visit their website to find out the specific requirements.

2. **Identify the Required Licenses:** Depending on your location, you may need a business license, animal control permit, zoning permit, and health department permit. Make a list of all the licenses and permits you need to apply for.

3. **Complete Application Forms:** Once you have identified the required licenses and permits, you will need to fill out the application forms. These forms typically require information about your business, such as the name, address, owner's information, and details about the kennel facilities.

4. **Submit Supporting Documents:** Along with the application forms, you may need to submit supporting documents such as a copy of your business plan, proof of insurance, zoning approval, and any other relevant paperwork. Make sure to include all the necessary documents to avoid delays in the application process.

5. **Pay Application Fees:** There are usually fees associated with applying for licenses and permits. Make sure to include the required fees with your application. The fees can vary depending on the type of license and the location of your kennel.

6. **Wait for Approval:** After submitting your application, you will need to wait for the licensing authorities to review and approve it. This process can take several weeks, so be patient and follow up with the authorities if necessary.

7. **Display Licenses:** Once you receive approval for your licenses and permits, make sure to display them prominently in your kennel facility. This will show your customers and authorities that your business is operating legally.

It is essential to comply with all licensing and permitting requirements to avoid fines, penalties, or even the closure of your business. By following these steps and ensuring that you have all the necessary licenses and permits, you can operate your kennel business smoothly and legally.

Chapter 10 - Obtain Necessary Business Licenses and Permits

Visit **www.BusinessBookstore.com/start** to download blank forms, etc.

Activity: Licenses and Permits Checklist

Before launching your business, it's essential to ensure that you have obtained all the necessary licenses and permits required to operate legally. Use the checklist below to track your progress and ensure compliance with regulatory requirements.

Remember to check with your local government offices or regulatory agencies to confirm the specific licenses and permits applicable to your business. Stay organized and proactive in fulfilling these requirements to avoid delays or penalties.

Once you have completed each item on this checklist, you can proceed with confidence, knowing that your business is compliant with all necessary licenses and permits.

This checklist serves as a comprehensive guide to help you navigate the process of obtaining licenses and permits for your business. By diligently completing each item, you're taking important steps towards ensuring legal compliance and operational readiness.

Licenses and Permits Checklist

- ☐ **Business Registration:** Register your business with the appropriate government authorities (e.g., state, county, city).

- ☐ **Professional Licenses:** Obtain any professional licenses required for your industry or profession (e.g., medical, legal, cosmetology).

- ☐ **Zoning Permits:** Check and obtain zoning permits to ensure your business location complies with local zoning regulations.

- ☐ **Health Department Permits:** Obtain health department permits if your business involves food handling, preparation, or serving.

- ☐ **Sales Tax Permit:** Apply for a sales tax permit if you will be selling goods or services subject to sales tax.

- ☐ **Alcohol and Tobacco Permits:** If applicable, obtain permits for selling alcohol or tobacco products.

- ☐ **Environmental Permits:** Obtain any necessary environmental permits if your business operations may impact the environment.

- ☐ **Building Permits:** Obtain building permits for any construction, renovations, or alterations to your business premises.

- ☐ **Signage Permits:** If installing signage, obtain permits from the local authorities as required.

- ☐ **Fire Department Permits:** Obtain permits related to fire safety and prevention for your business premises.

- ☐ **Occupational Safety and Health Administration (OSHA) Compliance:** Ensure compliance with OSHA regulations relevant to your industry and workplace safety.

- ☐ **Other Regulatory Approvals:** Identify and obtain any other specific licenses or permits required for your business operations.

Chapter 11

Select Your Business Location

> **Key Takeaways**
> - Assessing Location Needs and Preferences
> - Site Visits and Lease Negotiation
> - Activity: Location Evaluation Checklist

Choosing the right location for your kennel is a crucial decision that can significantly impact the success of your business. The location you select will not only affect your visibility and accessibility to customers but also influence your operating costs and overall profitability. As a small business owner, it is essential to carefully evaluate various factors before finalizing the location for your kennel.

When selecting a business location, it is important to consider your target market and their preferences. Understanding the demographics and psychographics of your potential customers can help you choose a location that is convenient and appealing to them. For example, if your target audience consists of busy professionals, you may want to consider locating your kennel in a commercial area with high foot traffic.

Additionally, you should assess the competition in the area and determine if there is a demand for your services. Conducting a thorough market analysis can help you identify gaps in the market and find a location that allows you to stand out from competitors. By understanding the competitive landscape, you can strategically position your kennel to attract customers and drive revenue.

Another important factor to consider when selecting a business location is the cost. Evaluate the rental or leasing rates in different areas and determine if they align with your budget and financial projections. It is crucial to strike a balance between affordability and potential profitability to ensure the long-term sustainability of your kennel.

Furthermore, you should assess the infrastructure and amenities available in the area to support your business operations. Consider factors such as parking facilities, accessibility for customers and employees, and proximity to suppliers and partners. Choosing a location with adequate infrastructure can enhance the efficiency of your kennel and create a positive experience for all stakeholders.

In this chapter, we will guide you through the process of selecting the ideal location for your kennel. From assessing your location needs and preferences to conducting site visits and negotiating lease agreements, we will provide you with practical tips and tools to make an informed decision. By the end of this chapter, you will have a clear understanding of how to choose a business location that sets your kennel up for success.

Remember, the location of your kennel plays a significant role in shaping your brand identity and customer perception. By carefully considering all the factors involved and making a well-informed decision, you can establish a strong foundation for your business and create a competitive advantage in the market. Let's get started on selecting the perfect location for your kennel!

Chapter 11 - Select Your Business Location

Assessing Location Needs and Preferences

When starting your own kennel, one of the most important decisions you will make is choosing the right location for your business. The location of your kennel can have a significant impact on its success, so it is crucial to carefully assess your needs and preferences before making a final decision.

Assessing Your Needs:

Before you start looking for a location, take some time to assess your needs. Consider factors such as the size of the space you require, the layout of the building, and any specific amenities or features that are important to you. For example, if you plan to offer grooming services, you will need a space with appropriate facilities. If you plan to offer boarding services, you will need separate areas for different types of animals.

It is also important to consider the needs of your customers. Think about factors such as convenience, accessibility, and parking availability. A location that is easy to find and has ample parking can attract more customers and make it easier for them to drop off and pick up their pets.

Assessing Your Preferences:

In addition to your needs, it is also important to consider your preferences when choosing a location for your kennel. Think about factors such as the overall look and feel of the area, the proximity to other businesses or attractions, and the potential for growth and expansion.

For example, you may prefer a location in a busy commercial area with high foot traffic, or you may prefer a quieter location in a residential neighborhood. Consider the atmosphere you want to create for your kennel and choose a location that aligns with your vision.

Examples and Suggestions:

Here are some examples and suggestions to help you assess your location needs and preferences:

- Visit potential locations in person to get a feel for the area and the surrounding neighborhood.
- Consider the demographics of the area and whether it aligns with your target audience.
- Research the local pet care market to see if there is demand for your services in the area.
- Think about the potential for growth and expansion in the area, and whether the location can accommodate your future plans.
- Consult with a real estate agent or business advisor to get professional advice on choosing the right location for your kennel.

By carefully assessing your needs and preferences, you can choose a location for your kennel that will set you up for success and help you achieve your business goals.

Chapter 11 - Select Your Business Location

Site Visits and Lease Negotiation

When starting your own kennel, choosing the right location is crucial for the success of your business. Conducting site visits and negotiating a lease are important steps in this process. Here are some key considerations to keep in mind:

1. **Assessing Location Needs and Preferences:** Before visiting potential sites, make a list of your specific requirements and preferences. Consider factors such as proximity to residential areas, accessibility for customers, zoning regulations, and space requirements for kennels, grooming areas, and outdoor facilities.

2. **Researching Potential Locations:** Once you have identified your criteria, start researching potential locations in your target area. Look for commercial real estate listings online, contact local real estate agents, and drive around the area to spot available properties.

3. **Setting Up Site Visits:** Contact the property owners or leasing agents to schedule site visits. During the visits, pay attention to the condition of the premises, the layout of the space, parking availability, and any potential renovations or improvements that may be needed.

4. **Asking the Right Questions:** Prepare a list of questions to ask during the site visits. Inquire about lease terms, rent prices, utilities, maintenance responsibilities, and any restrictions or limitations that may apply to the property.

5. **Negotiating Lease Terms:** Once you have found a location that meets your requirements, it's time to negotiate the lease agreement. Consider hiring a real estate attorney to help you review and negotiate the terms of the lease to ensure that they are favorable to your business.

6. **Understanding Lease Terms:** Make sure you understand all the terms and conditions of the lease, including rent amount, lease duration, renewal options, security deposit requirements, maintenance responsibilities, and any restrictions on modifications or subleasing.

7. **Securing the Lease:** Once you have reached an agreement with the landlord, review the lease agreement carefully before signing it. Make sure all agreed-upon terms are included in the contract and that you have a clear understanding of your rights and obligations as a tenant.

8. **Planning for Renovations:** If the property requires renovations or modifications to fit your needs, make sure to include these costs in your budget and timeline. Obtain necessary permits and approvals before starting any construction work.

9. **Considering Future Growth:** When choosing a location and negotiating a lease, consider the potential for future growth and expansion of your kennel business. Look for a space that can accommodate your long-term goals and business development plans.

Remember, the location of your kennel can have a significant impact on the success of your business. Take the time to visit potential sites, negotiate a favorable lease agreement, and plan for the future growth of your business.

Chapter 11 - Select Your Business Location

> Visit **www.BusinessBookstore.com/start** to download blank forms, etc.

Activity: Location Evaluation Checklist

Before finalizing your decision on a business location, it's crucial to thoroughly evaluate each potential site to ensure it aligns with your business needs and preferences. Use the following checklist during site visits to assess key factors and make an informed decision about the suitability of each location:

1. **Location and Accessibility:**

   ☐ Convenient proximity to target market

   ☐ Easy accessibility for customers and employees

   ☐ Visibility from main roads or thoroughfares

   ☐ Ample parking availability for customers and employees

2. **Physical Property Attributes:**

   ☐ Adequate space for current and future business needs

   ☐ Suitable layout and configuration for business operations

   ☐ Well-maintained condition of the property and facilities

   ☐ Compliance with zoning regulations and building codes

3. **Local Amenities and Infrastructure:**

    ☐ Availability of essential utilities (electricity, water, internet)

    ☐ Proximity to public transportation options, if applicable

    ☐ Access to amenities such as restaurants, banks, and other businesses

    ☐ Presence of supportive business infrastructure (business parks, incubators)

4. **Surrounding Environment and Community:**

    ☐ Compatibility with the overall aesthetic and vibe of the neighborhood

    ☐ Safety and security of the area, both during business hours and after-hours

    ☐ Presence of potential competitors and complementary businesses

    ☐ Engagement with the local community and potential for community support

5. **Lease Terms and Financial Considerations:**

    ☐ Affordability of rent and associated expenses (utilities, maintenance)

    ☐ Flexibility in lease terms (lease duration, renewal options)

    ☐ Transparency of lease agreements and any additional fees or charges

    ☐ Alignment with budgetary constraints and financial projection

6. **Landlord or Property Owner Relations:**

    ☐ Positive rapport and communication with the landlord or property owner
    ☐ Responsiveness to inquiries and concerns during the site visit
    ☐ Willingness to address potential issues and negotiate lease terms

7. **Overall Impression and Gut Feeling:**

    ☐ Personal gut feeling about the location's suitability for your business
    ☐ Overall impression of the property and its potential for success
    ☐ Alignment with your business's values, vision, and long-term goals

Once you have completed site visits and evaluated each potential location using this checklist, you will be better equipped to make an informed decision about the best location for your business.

Chapter 12 - Manage Suppliers and Inventory

Chapter 12

Manage Suppliers and Inventory

Key Takeaways

- Sourcing Suppliers and Negotiating Contracts
- Establishing Inventory Management Systems
- Activity: Supplier Evaluation Form

Welcome to Chapter 12 of 'How to Start Your Own Kennel'! In this chapter, we will discuss the importance of managing suppliers and inventory effectively for your kennel business. As a small business owner, it is crucial to establish strong relationships with suppliers and maintain an efficient inventory system to ensure the smooth operation of your kennel.

Managing suppliers involves sourcing the necessary products and services for your kennel, negotiating contracts, and maintaining good communication with your suppliers. By effectively managing your suppliers, you can ensure timely delivery of products, competitive pricing, and quality assurance for your kennel.

Inventory management is equally important as it involves tracking and controlling the goods and supplies that are essential for running your kennel. By implementing an efficient inventory system, you can prevent stockouts, reduce excess inventory, and optimize your cash flow.

Throughout this chapter, we will provide you with practical tips and strategies to help you manage your suppliers and inventory effectively. By following the guidelines and completing the activities in this chapter, you will be able to streamline your procurement process, minimize costs, and improve the overall efficiency of your kennel business.

Remember, managing suppliers and inventory is a continuous process that requires attention to detail and proactive planning. By investing time and effort into establishing strong supplier relationships and implementing robust inventory management practices, you can set your kennel business up for long-term success.

So, let's dive into Chapter 12 and learn how to effectively manage suppliers and inventory for your kennel business. By mastering these essential aspects of business operations, you will be one step closer to achieving your goals and building a thriving kennel business.

Chapter 12 - Manage Suppliers and Inventory

Sourcing Suppliers and Negotiating Contracts

When starting your own kennel, sourcing suppliers and negotiating contracts is a crucial step in ensuring that you have the necessary resources to run your business smoothly. Here are some key considerations to keep in mind:

1. **Identify Your Needs:** Before you start sourcing suppliers, it's important to identify your specific needs. This includes determining the types of products or services you require, the quantity needed, and the quality standards you expect. For a kennel, you may need suppliers for pet food, grooming supplies, bedding, and other essentials.

2. **Research Potential Suppliers:** Once you know your needs, research potential suppliers who can meet those requirements. Look for suppliers who have a good reputation, offer competitive pricing, and have a track record of reliability. You can search online, attend trade shows, or ask for recommendations from other pet business owners.

   - **Example:** If you need a supplier for pet food, consider reaching out to reputable pet food manufacturers or distributors in your area.

3. **Request Quotes and Proposals:** Reach out to potential suppliers and request quotes or proposals for the products or services you need. Compare pricing, quality, and terms offered by different suppliers to find the best fit for your business. Don't be afraid to negotiate on pricing or terms to get the best deal possible.

   - **Example:** When requesting quotes for grooming supplies, ask about bulk discounts or special promotions that may be available.

4. **Establish Relationships:** Building strong relationships with your suppliers is key to ensuring a smooth and reliable supply chain. Communicate openly with your suppliers, provide feedback on their products or services, and address any issues or concerns promptly. A good relationship with your suppliers can lead to better pricing, priority service, and other benefits.

   - **Example:** Consider scheduling regular meetings or check-ins with your suppliers to discuss upcoming needs and address any challenges.

5. **Negotiate Contracts:** Once you've chosen your suppliers, it's time to negotiate contracts that outline the terms of your partnership. Contracts should include details such as pricing, payment terms, delivery schedules, quality standards, and dispute resolution procedures. Make sure to review contracts carefully and seek legal advice if needed before signing.

   - **Example:** When negotiating a contract with a bedding supplier, clarify the expected delivery schedule, quality specifications, and payment terms to avoid any misunderstandings.

6. **Monitor Performance:** After establishing relationships and signing contracts, it's important to monitor your suppliers' performance regularly. Keep track of key performance indicators such as delivery times, product quality, and customer service. Address any issues or concerns promptly to ensure that your supply chain remains reliable.

   - **Example:** Create a supplier scorecard to evaluate and track your suppliers' performance over time, making it easier to identify areas for improvement.

Chapter 12 - Manage Suppliers and Inventory

By following these steps and taking a proactive approach to sourcing suppliers and negotiating contracts, you can build a strong and reliable supply chain for your kennel business. Remember to stay organized, communicate effectively, and prioritize building positive relationships with your suppliers to set your business up for success.

Establishing Inventory Management Systems

Establishing an effective inventory management system is crucial for the success of your kennel business. Proper inventory management ensures that you have the right products in stock at the right time, minimizing stockouts and overstock situations. Here are some key steps to help you set up an inventory management system:

1. **Assess Your Inventory Needs:** Start by taking stock of the items you currently have in your kennel, such as dog food, toys, grooming supplies, and other essentials. Determine which items are fast-moving and which ones are slow-moving to better understand your inventory needs.

2. **Choose an Inventory Management Method:** There are several inventory management methods you can choose from, such as First In, First Out (FIFO), Last In, First Out (LIFO), or Just In Time (JIT). Select a method that works best for your kennel business based on your inventory turnover rate and storage capacity.

3. **Invest in Inventory Management Software:** Consider investing in inventory management software to streamline your inventory tracking process. These tools can help you keep track of stock levels, reorder points, and supplier information, making it easier to manage your inventory effectively.

4. **Set Reorder Points:** Determine the minimum quantity of each item you should have in stock before placing a reorder. Setting reorder points can help prevent stockouts and ensure that you always have enough inventory on hand to meet customer demand.

5. **Implement Barcode Scanning:** Using barcode scanning technology can help you accurately track inventory levels and reduce human error. Barcode scanners can quickly scan items in and out of your inventory system, making it easier to keep track of stock movements.

6. **Establish Storage Procedures:** Organize your inventory in a systematic manner to make it easier to locate items when needed. Consider labeling shelves, bins, or storage areas to ensure that items are stored in the right place and can be easily accessed.

7. **Conduct Regular Inventory Audits:** Schedule regular inventory audits to reconcile physical inventory counts with your inventory records. This will help you identify any discrepancies or inaccuracies in your inventory data and take corrective actions as needed.

8. **Monitor Inventory Turnover:** Keep track of your inventory turnover rate to assess how quickly your inventory is moving. High turnover rates indicate that your products are selling well, while low turnover rates may signal slow-moving inventory that needs to be addressed.

9. **Optimize Order Fulfillment:** Streamline your order fulfillment process to ensure that customer orders are processed and shipped in a timely manner. Efficient order fulfillment can help improve customer satisfaction and loyalty.

10. **Review and Adjust Your Inventory Management System:** Regularly review your inventory management system to identify areas for improvement. Analyze key performance indicators such as stock levels, lead times, and order accuracy to make informed decisions and optimize your inventory management processes.

By following these steps and implementing an effective inventory management system, you can ensure that your kennel business runs smoothly and efficiently. Proper inventory management will help you minimize costs, improve customer satisfaction, and maximize profitability in the long run.

Chapter 12 - Manage Suppliers and Inventory

Visit **www.BusinessBookstore.com/start** for a list of suppliers.

Activity: Supplier Evaluation Form

Instructions:

Before selecting suppliers for your business, it's essential to thoroughly evaluate their capabilities, reliability, and compatibility with your business needs. Use the following Supplier Evaluation Form to assess potential suppliers based on key criteria discussed in previous chapters. Rate each criterion on a scale of 1 to 5, with 1 being the lowest and 5 being the highest, and provide comments or additional notes as needed. This evaluation will help you make informed decisions and choose suppliers that align with your business goals and requirements.

Supplier Evaluation Form

1. Supplier Information:

- Name of Supplier: _____

- Contact Person: _____

- Contact Information: _____

- Industry Experience: [Rating: 1-5] _____

    Comments: _____

- Reputation and References: [Rating: 1-5] _____

    Comments: _____

- Financial Stability: [Rating: 1-5] _____

    Comments: _____

© 2024 BusinessBookstore.com

2. Product Quality and Consistency:

- Quality Control Measures: [Rating: 1-5] _____

    Comments: _____

- Compliance with Standards: [Rating: 1-5] _____

    Comments: _____

- Product Warranty/Guarantee: [Rating: 1-5] _____

    Comments: _____

3. Price and Terms:

- Pricing Competitiveness: [Rating: 1-5] _____

    Comments: _____

- Payment Terms and Conditions: [Rating: 1-5] _____

    Comments: _____

- Volume Discounts: [Rating: 1-5] _____

    Comments: _____

4. Delivery and Lead Times:

- On-Time Delivery Performance: [Rating: 1-5] _____

    Comments: _____

- Lead Time for Orders: [Rating: 1-5] _____

    Comments: _____

Chapter 12 - Manage Suppliers and Inventory

- Shipping and Handling: [Rating: 1-5] _____

    Comments: _____

5. Customer Service and Support:

- Responsiveness to Inquiries: [Rating: 1-5] _____

    Comments: _____

- Problem Resolution: [Rating: 1-5] _____

    Comments: _____

- Availability of Support: [Rating: 1-5] _____

    Comments: _____

6. Overall Satisfaction:

- Overall Satisfaction with Supplier: [Rating: 1-5] _____

    Comments: _____

Conclusion:

After completing the Supplier Evaluation Form for each potential supplier, review the ratings and comments to identify strengths, weaknesses, and areas for improvement. Use this information to make informed decisions about selecting suppliers that best meet your business requirements and objectives. Remember to revisit and update the evaluation periodically to ensure ongoing supplier performance and satisfaction.

Chapter 13 - Protect Your Business with Insurance

Chapter 13

Protect Your Business With Insurance

Key Takeaways

- Understanding Business Insurance Needs
- Choosing the Right Insurance Policies
- Activity: Business Insurance Checklist

As a small business owner, you have put your heart and soul into building your kennel from the ground up. You have invested time, money, and effort into creating a safe and welcoming environment for your furry clients. But have you considered how you would protect your business in the event of unforeseen circumstances?

Insurance is a crucial aspect of running a successful kennel business. It provides you with a safety net in case of accidents, lawsuits, or other unexpected events that could potentially threaten the future of your business. By having the right insurance coverage in place, you can safeguard your assets, protect your employees, and ensure the longevity of your kennel.

Many small business owners overlook the importance of insurance, thinking that it is an unnecessary expense or that they are not at risk of facing any liabilities. However, the reality is that accidents can happen at any time, and without the proper insurance coverage, you could be putting your business at great risk.

Insurance not only protects your business assets but also gives you peace of mind knowing that you are prepared for any challenges that may come your way. Whether it's property damage, employee injuries, or customer lawsuits, having the right insurance coverage can help you weather the storm and continue operating your kennel business successfully.

In this chapter, we will explore the different types of insurance policies that are essential for kennel owners, including general liability insurance, property insurance, workers' compensation insurance, and more. We will discuss the importance of each type of coverage and how it can benefit your business in the long run.

It is important to remember that insurance is not just a legal requirement but a strategic investment in the future of your business. By taking the time to understand your insurance needs and choosing the right policies for your kennel, you can protect your business from potential risks and liabilities that could otherwise derail your success.

So, as you embark on this journey of starting your own kennel business, remember to prioritize insurance as a key component of your overall risk management strategy. It may seem like a small detail now, but having the right insurance coverage in place can make all the difference in the long-term success and sustainability of your business.

Let's dive into the world of insurance and learn how you can protect your business with the right coverage. Together, we will ensure that your kennel is well-prepared for whatever challenges may come your way, allowing you to focus on what you do best, caring for our beloved four-legged friends.

Chapter 13 - Protect Your Business with Insurance

Understanding Business Insurance Needs

When starting your own kennel, one of the most important aspects to consider is business insurance. Business insurance is essential for protecting your kennel from potential risks and liabilities that may arise in the course of running your business.

Understanding Business Insurance Needs:

1. **Types of Business Insurance:** There are several types of insurance policies that you may need to consider for your kennel:

    - **General Liability Insurance:** This type of insurance provides coverage for third-party bodily injury, property damage, and advertising injury claims. It is essential for protecting your kennel from lawsuits and legal claims.

    - **Property Insurance:** Property insurance covers damage or loss to your kennel property, including buildings, equipment, and supplies. It is important to ensure that your property is adequately covered in case of fire, theft, or other disasters.

    - **Professional Liability Insurance:** Also known as errors and omissions insurance, this policy provides coverage for claims of negligence or mistakes in your professional services. If a client accuses you of providing inadequate care for their pet, professional liability insurance can help cover legal costs and damages.

    - **Workers' Compensation Insurance:** If you have employees working at your kennel, you may be required by law to carry workers' compensation insurance. This policy provides coverage for medical expenses and lost wages for employees who are injured on the job.

2. **Assessing Risks:** Before purchasing insurance policies for your kennel, it is important to assess the potential risks that your business may face. Consider factors such as the size of your kennel, the number of employees, the types of services you offer, and the location of your business. By identifying potential risks, you can select insurance policies that provide adequate coverage for your specific needs.

3. **Consulting with an Insurance Agent:** To ensure that you have the right insurance coverage for your kennel, it is recommended to consult with an insurance agent who specializes in small business insurance. An insurance agent can assess your needs, recommend appropriate policies, and help you navigate the complexities of insurance coverage.

4. **Reviewing Policy Limits and Exclusions:** When purchasing insurance policies for your kennel, it is important to review the policy limits and exclusions carefully. Make sure that the coverage limits are sufficient to protect your business assets and that there are no significant exclusions that could leave you vulnerable to certain risks.

5. **Updating Insurance Coverage:** As your kennel grows and evolves, it is important to regularly review and update your insurance coverage. Changes in your business operations, services, or number of employees may require adjustments to your insurance policies to ensure that you are adequately protected.

By understanding your business insurance needs and selecting the right insurance policies for your kennel, you can protect your business from potential risks and liabilities. Investing in comprehensive insurance coverage is a proactive step towards safeguarding your kennel's financial stability and reputation.

Chapter 13 - Protect Your Business with Insurance

Choosing the Right Insurance Policies

When starting your own kennel, one of the most important steps you can take to protect your business is to choose the right insurance policies. Insurance is essential for safeguarding your assets, employees, and customers in case of unforeseen events or accidents. Here are some key considerations to keep in mind when selecting insurance policies for your kennel:

1. **General Liability Insurance:** This type of insurance is crucial for any business, including kennels. General liability insurance protects you in case someone is injured on your property or if there is property damage as a result of your business operations. It can also cover legal fees in case of a lawsuit.

2. **Property Insurance:** Property insurance is essential for protecting your physical assets, such as your kennel building, equipment, and supplies. Make sure to accurately assess the value of your property to ensure you have adequate coverage in case of damage or loss.

3. **Workers' Compensation Insurance:** If you have employees working at your kennel, you are required by law to have workers' compensation insurance. This type of insurance provides coverage for medical expenses and lost wages for employees who are injured on the job.

4. **Professional Liability Insurance:** Also known as errors and omissions insurance, professional liability insurance protects you in case a customer claims that your services or advice led to financial loss or harm. This type of insurance is especially important for businesses that provide pet care services.

5. **Business Interruption Insurance:** Business interruption insurance provides coverage for lost income and expenses in case your kennel is forced to close temporarily due to a covered event, such as a natural disaster. This insurance can help you stay afloat during a difficult time.

6. **Cyber Liability Insurance:** In today's digital age, cyber liability insurance is becoming increasingly important for businesses that store sensitive customer information electronically. This type of insurance can help cover the costs associated with a data breach or cyberattack.

When selecting insurance policies for your kennel, it's important to work with an experienced insurance agent who understands the unique risks associated with your business. Consider obtaining quotes from multiple insurance providers to compare coverage options and premiums. Remember that the cheapest policy may not always provide the best coverage, so be sure to carefully review the terms and conditions of each policy before making a decision.

Additionally, regularly review your insurance coverage to ensure it aligns with the evolving needs of your kennel. As your business grows and changes, you may need to adjust your insurance policies accordingly to adequately protect your assets and mitigate risks.

By choosing the right insurance policies for your kennel, you can protect your business from potential liabilities and ensure its long-term success.

Chapter 13 - Protect Your Business with Insurance

Visit **www.BusinessBookstore.com/start** for a list of insurance agencies.

Activity: Business Insurance Checklist

Assess Your Insurance Needs

Identify Potential Risks

- ☐ List the types of risks your business may face (e.g., property damage, liability, employee injuries).
- ☐ Consider industry-specific risks.

Evaluate Coverage Requirements

- ☐ Determine which types of insurance are legally required in your location (e.g., workers' compensation).
- ☐ Identify additional coverage that might be beneficial (e.g., cyber liability insurance).

Research Insurance Providers

Compare Multiple Providers

- ☐ List at least three insurance providers you will consider.
- ☐ Check each provider's reputation and customer reviews.

Request Quotes

- ☐ Obtain detailed quotes from each provider for the types of coverage you need.
- ☐ Ensure quotes include coverage limits, deductibles, and premiums.

Evaluate Insurance Policies

Coverage Options

- ☐ Compare the types of coverage offered by each provider.
- ☐ Ensure policies cover all identified risks and requirements.

Policy Terms and Conditions

- ☐ Review exclusions and limitations in each policy.
- ☐ Check for any additional fees or clauses that could impact coverage.

Make a Decision

Cost vs. Coverage

- ☐ Balance the cost of premiums against the level of coverage provided.
- ☐ Consider any potential discounts for bundling policies.

Provider Reliability

- ☐ Evaluate the reliability and financial stability of each provider.
- ☐ Consider the provider's customer service and claims handling process.

Purchase and Review

Select Your Policies

- ☐ Choose the insurance policies that best meet your business needs.
- ☐ Ensure you understand the coverage details and terms.

Regularly Review Coverage

- ☐ Set reminders to review your insurance coverage annually.
- ☐ Adjust policies as your business grows or changes.

Chapter 14

Hire and Train Your Team

> **Key Takeaways**
> - Identifying Hiring Needs and Job Roles
> - Recruiting and Interviewing Candidates
> - Activity: Hiring Process Checklist

As a small business owner, one of the most important decisions you will make is hiring and training your team. Your employees are the backbone of your kennel business, and having the right people in place can make all the difference in your success. In this chapter, we will discuss the key steps and strategies for hiring and training a team that will help you achieve your business goals.

Identifying Hiring Needs and Job Roles

Before you begin the hiring process, it's essential to identify your staffing needs and determine the roles and responsibilities you need to fill. Consider the tasks that need to be completed on a daily basis, as well as any long-term goals you have for your kennel business. This will help you create job descriptions and qualifications for each position you are looking to fill.

Recruiting and Interviewing Candidates

Once you have a clear understanding of the roles you need to fill, it's time to start recruiting candidates. There are many ways to find potential employees, including job boards, social media, and employee referrals. When interviewing candidates, be sure to ask questions that will help you assess their skills, experience, and fit with your company culture. It's also important to conduct thorough background checks and reference checks to ensure you are hiring the best candidates for your team.

Activity: Hiring Process Checklist

Use the checklist provided in this chapter to guide you through the hiring process. This checklist will help you stay organized and ensure you are following best practices when recruiting, interviewing, and hiring new employees for your kennel business.

Hiring and training a team can be a challenging but rewarding process. By taking the time to identify your hiring needs, recruit top talent, and provide thorough training, you can build a team that will help your kennel business thrive. Remember, your employees are your most valuable asset, so invest in them and set them up for success.

Chapter 14 - Hire and Train Your Team

Identifying Hiring Needs and Job Roles

When starting your own kennel, one of the most important aspects to consider is identifying the hiring needs and job roles within your business. This step is crucial in ensuring that you have the right team in place to help you achieve your business goals and provide excellent service to your customers. In this section, we will discuss how to identify the hiring needs of your kennel and define the various job roles that will be essential to the success of your business.

Identifying Hiring Needs:

Before you can begin hiring employees for your kennel, it is important to assess your business needs and determine the areas where additional help is required. Consider the size of your kennel, the services you plan to offer, and the number of customers you expect to serve on a daily basis. This will help you identify the specific roles that need to be filled within your business.

For example, if you plan to offer grooming services in addition to boarding and daycare, you may need to hire professional groomers with experience in handling different breeds of dogs. If you anticipate a high volume of customers, you may also need to hire additional staff to help with customer service, cleaning, and administrative tasks.

It is also important to consider the skills and qualifications that are necessary for each role. For example, employees who will be interacting with dogs on a daily basis should have experience working with animals and a genuine love for pets. Administrative staff should have strong organizational skills and attention to detail.

Defining Job Roles:

Once you have identified the hiring needs of your kennel, the next step is to define the specific job roles that will need to be filled. This involves creating job descriptions that outline the responsibilities, qualifications, and expectations for each position within your business.

For example, a job description for a dog daycare attendant may include responsibilities such as supervising playtime, feeding and watering dogs, and monitoring behavior for signs of aggression or illness. Qualifications for this role may include experience working with dogs, knowledge of dog behavior, and the ability to handle multiple dogs at once.

Similarly, a job description for a customer service representative may include responsibilities such as answering phones, scheduling appointments, and addressing customer inquiries and concerns. Qualifications for this role may include excellent communication skills, a friendly and outgoing personality, and the ability to multitask in a fast-paced environment.

It is important to be clear and specific when defining job roles to ensure that potential candidates understand the expectations of the position and can determine if they are a good fit for the role. This will also help you attract qualified candidates who are well-suited to the demands of the job.

Chapter 14 - Hire and Train Your Team

Conclusion:

Identifying hiring needs and defining job roles are essential steps in building a successful team for your kennel. By assessing your business needs, determining the specific roles that need to be filled, and creating clear job descriptions, you can ensure that you hire employees who are qualified, competent, and dedicated to providing excellent service to your customers. Remember to consider the skills and qualifications required for each role, and to be clear and specific when outlining job responsibilities and expectations. With the right team in place, your kennel will be well-equipped to provide top-notch care and service to the furry friends in your community.

Recruiting and Interviewing Candidates

Recruiting and interviewing candidates is a crucial step in building your kennel team. Finding the right people who are passionate about animals and dedicated to providing excellent care is essential for the success of your business. Here are some tips and best practices to help you navigate the recruitment and interview process:

1. **Define the Job Requirements:** Before you start recruiting, clearly define the roles and responsibilities of the positions you are looking to fill. Consider the skills, experience, and qualifications needed to perform the job effectively.

2. **Write a Compelling Job Description:** Craft a job description that accurately reflects the responsibilities of the role and highlights the unique aspects of working at your kennel. Be sure to include information about your company culture, values, and any benefits or perks offered.

3. **Utilize Multiple Recruitment Channels:** To reach a wider pool of candidates, consider using a mix of recruitment channels such as job boards, social media, industry-specific websites, and local community boards. Networking with other pet care professionals can also be a valuable source of referrals.

4. **Screen Resumes and Applications:** Review resumes and applications carefully to identify candidates who meet the job requirements. Look for relevant experience, qualifications, and a genuine passion for working with animals.

5. **Conduct Phone Interviews:** Before inviting candidates for in-person interviews, conduct phone interviews to assess their communication skills, enthusiasm for the role, and availability. Use this opportunity to ask preliminary questions and gauge their interest in the position.

Chapter 14 - Hire and Train Your Team

6. **Prepare for In-Person Interviews:** Develop a list of interview questions that will help you evaluate candidates' skills, experience, and fit with your kennel's culture. Consider asking scenario-based questions to assess their problem-solving abilities and their approach to handling challenging situations.

7. **Showcase Your Kennel:** During the interview, take the time to showcase your kennel and share information about your services, values, and team dynamics. Help candidates envision themselves as part of your team and demonstrate your commitment to providing a positive work environment.

8. **Assess Cultural Fit:** In addition to evaluating candidates' technical skills, pay attention to their personality, attitude, and values. Look for individuals who align with your company culture, share your passion for animals, and demonstrate a strong work ethic.

9. **Ask for References:** Before making a hiring decision, request references from previous employers or colleagues to validate the candidate's qualifications and work ethic. Contacting references can provide valuable insights into their performance and reliability.

10. **Follow Up with Candidates:** After the interviews, follow up with candidates to thank them for their time and provide feedback on the interview process. Keep communication open and transparent to maintain a positive candidate experience, even if they are not selected for the position.

By following these recruitment and interviewing best practices, you can attract top talent to join your kennel team and contribute to the success of your business. Remember that building a strong team of dedicated and passionate individuals is key to providing exceptional care for the animals in your care.

Chapter 14 - Hire and Train Your Team

> Visit **www.BusinessBookstore.com/start** to download blank staffing forms.

Activity: Hiring Process Checklist

Congratulations on taking the next step in building your dream team! Use this checklist to guide you through the hiring process and ensure you find the best candidates for your small business.

1. **Define Hiring Needs:**

    ☐ Identify the roles and positions you need to fill.

    ☐ Determine the qualifications, skills, and experience required for each role.

    ☐ Set clear objectives and expectations for the new hires.

2. **Craft Job Descriptions:**

    ☐ Write clear and concise job descriptions for each role.

    ☐ Highlight the responsibilities, qualifications, and key competencies required.

    ☐ Include information about your company culture, values, and mission to attract the right candidates.

3. **Choose Recruitment Channels:**

    ☐ Select appropriate recruitment channels such as job boards, social media, and professional networks.

    ☐ Utilize employee referrals and networking to reach potential candidates.

    ☐ Consider using recruitment agencies or outsourcing if needed.

4. **Screen Resumes and Applications:**

    ☐ Review resumes, cover letters, and applications to shortlist qualified candidates.
    ☐ Look for relevant skills, experience, and alignment with your company culture.
    ☐ Keep track of candidates' information and communication for future reference.

5. **Conduct Interviews:**

    ☐ Schedule interviews with shortlisted candidates.

    ☐ Prepare a list of structured interview questions tailored to each role.
    ☐ Conduct interviews to assess candidates' qualifications, experience, and cultural fit.

6. **Assess Candidates:**

    ☐ Evaluate candidates based on their skills, experience, and alignment with your company values.
    ☐ Consider conducting additional assessments or tests if necessary.
    ☐ Gather feedback from other team members involved in the interview process.

7. **Extend Job Offers:**

    ☐ Select the top candidate for each role.

    ☐ Prepare and extend job offers to selected candidates.

    ☐ Negotiate terms of employment, including salary, benefits, and start date.

8. **Onboarding Process:**

    ☐ Develop an onboarding plan to welcome new hires and integrate them into your team.
    ☐ Provide necessary training, resources, and support to help new hires succeed.
    ☐ Communicate expectations and goals for the new hires' roles.

9. **Follow-Up and Feedback:**

    ☐ Follow up with candidates who were not selected and provide constructive feedback if possible.
    ☐ Monitor the performance and progress of new hires during their probationary period.
    ☐ Seek feedback from new hires to continuously improve your hiring process.

10. **Continuous Improvement:**

    ☐ Reflect on the hiring process and identify areas for improvement.
    ☐ Solicit feedback from your team and candidates to enhance the recruitment experience.
    ☐ Update job descriptions, interview questions, and recruitment strategies based on lessons learned.

Remember to customize this checklist to fit your specific hiring needs and adapt it as your small business grows and evolves. Good luck with your hiring process!

Chapter 15

Set Up Your Technology

> **Key Takeaways**
> - Assessing Technology Requirements
> - Selecting Software and Tools
> - Activity: Technology Needs Assessment

Welcome to Chapter 15 of 'How to Start Your Own Kennel'! In this chapter, we will discuss the importance of setting up technology for your new business. As a small business owner, embracing technology is essential for staying competitive in today's digital age. By leveraging the right tools and software, you can streamline your operations, improve efficiency, and enhance customer experience.

Setting up technology for your kennel may seem daunting, especially if you're not tech-savvy. However, with the right guidance and resources, you can navigate this process successfully. Whether you're looking to manage bookings, track inventory, or communicate with customers, there are a variety of technology solutions available to meet your specific needs.

As you embark on this journey of setting up your technology infrastructure, keep in mind that the goal is to simplify your daily tasks and empower your business to grow. By investing in the right technology tools, you can position your kennel for success and create a seamless experience for both your team and your customers.

Throughout this chapter, we will cover key topics such as assessing your technology requirements, selecting the right software and tools, and creating a plan for implementation. By following the steps outlined in this chapter, you can ensure that your kennel is equipped with the necessary technology to thrive in today's competitive market.

Remember, technology is not just a luxury for large corporations, it is a necessity for businesses of all sizes. By embracing technology and incorporating it into your daily operations, you can set your kennel apart from the competition and position yourself for long-term success.

So, whether you're a tech novice or a seasoned pro, this chapter will provide you with the guidance and resources you need to set up your technology infrastructure effectively. By taking the time to invest in the right tools and systems, you can create a solid foundation for your kennel and pave the way for future growth and success.

Now, let's dive into the world of technology and discover how you can leverage it to take your kennel to new heights!

Chapter 15 - Set Up Your Technology

Assessing Technology Requirements

When starting your own kennel, it's essential to assess your technology requirements to ensure smooth operations and efficient management of your business. Technology plays a crucial role in modern businesses, including kennels, as it can help streamline processes, improve customer service, and enhance overall productivity.

Here are some key steps to consider when assessing your technology requirements for your kennel:

1. **Identify Your Needs:** Start by identifying the specific areas in your kennel where technology can be beneficial. This could include software for booking appointments, managing inventory, tracking customer information, or even monitoring the health and well-being of the animals in your care.

2. **Research Available Solutions:** Once you have identified your needs, research the available technology solutions in the market that can address those needs. Look for software providers that specialize in pet care businesses or kennel management systems.

3. **Consider Cloud-Based Solutions:** Cloud-based software solutions offer flexibility and accessibility, allowing you to manage your kennel operations from anywhere with an internet connection. This can be particularly useful if you have multiple locations or if you need to access information on the go.

4. **Invest in Quality Hardware:** In addition to software, consider the hardware requirements for your kennel, such as computers, tablets, or mobile devices. Ensure that your hardware is reliable and up to date to support the software applications you plan to use.

5. **Think About Security:** Protecting sensitive information, such as customer data or financial records, is crucial for any business. Consider investing in cybersecurity measures, such as firewalls, antivirus software, and data encryption, to safeguard your kennel's digital assets.

Here are some examples of technology solutions that you may want to consider for your kennel:

- **Appointment Scheduling Software:** Use a scheduling system that allows customers to book appointments online and helps you manage your kennel's daily schedule efficiently.

- **Inventory Management System:** Keep track of your supplies, food, and medications with an inventory management system that alerts you when stock is running low.

- **Customer Relationship Management (CRM) Software:** Manage customer information, preferences, and communication with a CRM system that helps you provide personalized service and build customer loyalty.

- **Security Cameras and Monitoring Systems:** Install cameras and monitoring systems to ensure the safety and security of the animals in your care, as well as to monitor staff activities.

By carefully assessing your technology requirements and investing in the right solutions, you can set your kennel up for success and provide a seamless experience for both your customers and your furry guests.

Chapter 15 - Set Up Your Technology

Selecting Software and Tools

When starting your own kennel, selecting the right software and tools is essential for running your business efficiently and effectively. There are a variety of options available to help you manage different aspects of your kennel, from booking appointments to tracking inventory. Here are some key considerations to keep in mind when choosing software and tools for your kennel:

1. **Identify Your Needs:** Before you start looking for software and tools, it's important to identify your specific needs. Consider what tasks you need help with, such as managing appointments, tracking customer information, or handling payments. Make a list of the features you require to streamline your operations.

2. **Research Options:** Once you have a clear understanding of your needs, research different software and tools that are available in the market. Look for solutions that are specifically designed for pet care businesses or kennels. Read reviews, compare features, and consider the pricing of each option.

3. **Consider Cloud-Based Solutions:** Cloud-based software offers the advantage of accessibility from anywhere with an internet connection. This can be particularly useful for managing your kennel on-the-go or allowing your staff to access information remotely. Consider cloud-based options for increased flexibility.

4. **Look for Integration Capabilities:** Choose software and tools that can integrate with each other to create a seamless workflow. For example, you may want your appointment scheduling software to sync with your customer database or your inventory management system. Integration can save you time and reduce errors.

5. **Prioritize Ease of Use:** Opt for software and tools that are user-friendly and intuitive. Your staff should be able to quickly learn how to use the system without extensive training. A simple interface can improve efficiency and reduce the likelihood of errors.

6. **Consider Mobile Accessibility:** In today's digital age, many businesses benefit from mobile accessibility. Look for software and tools that offer mobile apps or responsive design for easy access on smartphones and tablets. This can be especially helpful for managing appointments or communicating with customers on-the-go.

7. **Seek Customer Support:** Choose software providers that offer reliable customer support. In case you encounter any issues or have questions about the system, having access to a responsive support team can be invaluable. Check reviews and testimonials to gauge the level of customer service provided.

8. **Test Before Committing:** Before making a final decision, consider testing out a few software options to see which one best meets your needs. Many providers offer free trials or demos that allow you to explore the features and functionality of the software before making a purchase. Take advantage of these opportunities to ensure the software is the right fit for your kennel.

Examples of Software and Tools:

- *Appointment Scheduling:* Consider using software like PetDesk or Gingr to manage appointments, send reminders to customers, and track scheduling.

- *Customer Relationship Management (CRM):* Tools like PawLoyalty or Gingr can help you keep track of customer information, preferences, and communication history.

Chapter 15 - Set Up Your Technology

- **Inventory Management:** Look into software such as Brightpearl or Lightspeed to track inventory levels, manage suppliers, and streamline purchasing.

- **Payment Processing:** Consider using tools like Square or Stripe for secure and convenient payment processing options for your customers.

Chapter 15 - Set Up Your Technology

> Visit **www.BusinessBookstore.com/start** for a list of software providers.

Activity: Technology Needs Assessment

Before selecting software and tools for your small business, it's essential to assess your technology needs and requirements. Use the following checklist to evaluate your current technology infrastructure and identify areas where new software solutions could improve efficiency and support your business goals.

1. **Current Technology Infrastructure:**

    - ☐ Assess the current technology tools and systems used in your business, including hardware, software, and networking equipment.
    - ☐ Identify any gaps or limitations in your existing technology infrastructure that may be hindering productivity or growth.

2. **Business Goals and Objectives:**

    - ☐ Define your business goals and objectives, including short-term and long-term targets for growth, revenue, and customer satisfaction.
    - ☐ Determine how technology can support your business goals and enhance your ability to achieve success.

3. **Operational Needs and Challenges:**

    - ☐ Identify specific operational needs and challenges within your business, such as inventory management, customer relationship management, or financial reporting.
    - ☐ Consider how technology solutions can address these operational needs and challenges to streamline workflows and improve efficiency.

4. **Employee Requirements:**

    ☐ Evaluate the technology requirements of your employees, including software tools and systems needed to perform their roles effectively.
    ☐ Consider factors such as remote work capabilities, collaboration tools, and training needs to support your workforce.

5. **Customer Experience:**

    ☐ Assess the current customer experience provided by your business, including interactions through various channels such as your website, social media, and customer service.
    ☐ Identify opportunities to enhance the customer experience through technology solutions such as e-commerce platforms, customer relationship management (CRM) software, or communication tools.

6. **Security and Data Protection:**

    ☐ Review your current security measures and protocols to protect sensitive business data and customer information.
    ☐ Identify any potential vulnerabilities or areas of concern that need to be addressed with technology solutions such as cybersecurity software or data encryption tools.

7. **Budget and Resources:**

    ☐ Determine your budget and resources available for investing in new technology solutions.
    ☐ Consider factors such as upfront costs, ongoing maintenance fees, and potential return on investment (ROI) when evaluating technology options.

Chapter 15 - Set Up Your Technology

8. **Integration and Scalability:**

    ☐ Assess the compatibility and integration capabilities of potential technology solutions with your existing systems and tools.
    ☐ Consider the scalability of the software and tools to accommodate future growth and expansion of your business.

9. **Vendor Selection Criteria:**

    ☐ Define criteria for selecting technology vendors, including factors such as reputation, reliability, customer support, and user satisfaction.
    ☐ Research potential vendors and evaluate them against your selection criteria to identify the best fit for your business.

10. **Final Assessment and Prioritization:**

    ☐ Review your technology needs assessment and prioritize areas where new technology solutions are most needed and will have the greatest impact on your business.
    ☐ Develop a plan for implementing new technology solutions based on your assessment and prioritize them according to your business goals and objectives.

Conclusion:

Completing this technology needs assessment will provide valuable insights into your business's technology requirements and help you make informed decisions when selecting software and tools to support your operations. Use the information gathered from this assessment to guide your technology strategy and investment decisions for optimal business performance and growth.

Chapter 16

Prepare Your Launch Plan

> **Key Takeaways**
>
> - Setting Launch Goals and Objectives
> - Creating Launch Timeline and Marketing Strategy
> - Activity: Business Launch Checklist

Welcome to Chapter 16 of 'How to Start Your Own Kennel'! Congratulations on reaching this stage in your journey to starting your own business. In this chapter, we will focus on preparing a launch plan for your kennel. This is a crucial step in ensuring a successful launch and building a strong foundation for your business.

Launching a new business can be both exciting and challenging. It requires careful planning, organization, and attention to detail. A well-thought-out launch plan will help you introduce your kennel to the market effectively, attract customers, and generate buzz around your brand.

As a small business owner, it's essential to approach the launch of your kennel with enthusiasm and determination. This is your opportunity to showcase your passion for dogs, your expertise in the industry, and the unique value proposition of your business. A successful launch can set the tone for the future success of your kennel and establish a strong presence in the market.

Throughout this chapter, we will guide you through the process of preparing a comprehensive launch plan for your kennel. We will help you set clear goals and objectives, create a timeline for your launch activities, and develop a marketing strategy to promote your business effectively. By following the steps outlined in this chapter, you will be well-equipped to execute a successful launch and make a memorable first impression on your target audience.

Remember, the launch of your kennel is an opportunity to showcase your brand, connect with your customers, and establish your presence in the market. It's a chance to demonstrate why your kennel is unique, valuable, and worth their attention. With the right planning and execution, you can create a launch that resonates with your audience and sets your business up for long-term success.

So, get ready to roll up your sleeves and dive into the exciting world of launching your own kennel. Let's work together to create a launch plan that will captivate your audience, drive interest in your business, and pave the way for a bright future ahead. Are you ready to make your mark in the pet care industry? Let's get started!

Chapter 16 - Prepare Your Launch Plan

Setting Launch Goals and Objectives

Setting launch goals and objectives is a crucial step in preparing for the successful start of your kennel business. These goals and objectives will guide your planning and help you stay focused on what you want to achieve. In this section, we will discuss how to set effective launch goals and objectives for your kennel business.

1. **Define Your Goals:** Start by defining what you want to accomplish with the launch of your kennel business. Your goals should be specific, measurable, achievable, relevant, and time-bound (SMART). For example, your goals could include reaching a certain number of customers in the first month, generating a specific amount of revenue, or gaining a certain percentage of market share.

2. **Identify Key Objectives:** Once you have defined your goals, break them down into smaller, actionable objectives. These objectives should outline the steps you need to take to achieve your goals. For instance, if your goal is to reach a certain number of customers, your objectives could include launching a marketing campaign, setting up a customer referral program, and hosting a grand opening event.

3. **Prioritize Your Goals and Objectives:** It's essential to prioritize your goals and objectives to focus your efforts on what matters most. Consider the impact and feasibility of each goal and objective and rank them accordingly. Start with the goals and objectives that will have the most significant impact on your kennel business's success.

4. **Set Clear Metrics:** To measure the success of your launch goals and objectives, establish clear metrics that you can track and evaluate. These metrics could include the number of new customers acquired, revenue generated, social media engagement, website traffic, and customer satisfaction ratings. Regularly monitor these metrics to assess your progress and make adjustments as needed.

5. **Create a Timeline:** Develop a timeline that outlines when you will achieve each goal and objective. Break down your goals and objectives into smaller tasks and assign deadlines for each task. Having a timeline will help you stay on track and ensure that you are making progress towards your launch goals.

6. **Align Goals with Your Brand and Values:** Ensure that your launch goals and objectives align with your kennel business's brand identity and values. Your goals should reflect what sets your kennel apart from competitors and resonate with your target audience. For example, if one of your brand values is providing exceptional customer service, your goals and objectives should focus on delivering a superior customer experience.

7. **Stay Flexible:** While it's essential to set clear goals and objectives, it's also crucial to remain flexible and adapt to changing circumstances. Be open to revising your goals and objectives if necessary and be willing to pivot your strategy if things are not going as planned. Stay agile and responsive to ensure the success of your kennel business launch.

8. **Celebrate Milestones:** As you achieve your launch goals and objectives, take the time to celebrate your accomplishments. Recognize the hard work and dedication that went into reaching each milestone and reward yourself and your team for a job well done. Celebrating milestones will boost morale and motivate you to continue striving for success.

Chapter 16 - Prepare Your Launch Plan

Setting launch goals and objectives is a critical part of launching a successful kennel business. By defining your goals, identifying key objectives, prioritizing tasks, setting clear metrics, creating a timeline, aligning goals with your brand, staying flexible, and celebrating milestones, you can set yourself up for a successful launch and long-term success.

Creating Launch Timeline and Marketing Strategy

Creating a launch timeline and marketing strategy is crucial for the success of your kennel business. A well-thought-out plan will help you generate buzz, attract customers, and drive sales from day one. Here are some steps to consider when developing your launch timeline and marketing strategy:

1. **Set Clear Goals and Objectives:** Before you start planning your launch, it's essential to define your goals and objectives. What do you want to achieve with your launch? Are you looking to increase brand awareness, drive sales, or build a loyal customer base? Setting clear goals will help you tailor your marketing strategy accordingly.

2. **Identify Your Target Audience:** Understanding your target audience is key to creating a successful marketing strategy. Who are your ideal customers? What are their needs, preferences, and behaviors? By identifying your target audience, you can tailor your messaging and marketing channels to reach them effectively.

3. **Develop a Budget:** Determine how much you're willing to spend on your launch marketing efforts. Consider allocating funds for advertising, promotions, social media campaigns, and any other marketing activities that will help you reach your target audience.

4. **Create a Timeline:** Outline a timeline for your launch, starting from the pre-launch phase to the post-launch phase. Include key milestones, deadlines, and tasks that need to be completed before, during, and after the launch. A detailed timeline will help you stay organized and on track.

5. **Pre-Launch Marketing:** Build anticipation for your kennel business by creating a buzz before the official launch. Consider running teaser campaigns, hosting exclusive events, or offering pre-launch discounts to generate excitement among your target audience.

6. **Launch Day Activities:** Plan a series of activities and events to mark the official launch of your kennel business. This could include a grand opening ceremony, special promotions, giveaways, or contests to attract customers and drive foot traffic to your location.

7. **Post-Launch Marketing:** Keep the momentum going after the launch by continuing to engage with your customers. Consider running post-launch promotions, hosting customer appreciation events, or launching loyalty programs to encourage repeat business.

8. **Marketing Channels:** Determine which marketing channels will be most effective in reaching your target audience. This could include a mix of online and offline channels such as social media, email marketing, local advertising, and community outreach.

9. **Measure and Evaluate:** Track the performance of your launch marketing efforts by monitoring key metrics such as website traffic, social media engagement, sales conversions, and customer feedback. Use this data to evaluate the success of your launch strategy and make adjustments as needed.

By following these steps and creating a comprehensive launch timeline and marketing strategy, you'll be well-positioned to make a splash with your kennel business launch and set the stage for long-term success.

Chapter 16 - Prepare Your Launch Plan

> Visit **www.BusinessBookstore.com/start** to download blank forms, etc.

Activity: Business Launch Checklist

Congratulations on reaching the final stage of preparing for your business launch! This checklist will serve as a comprehensive guide to ensure that you have covered all the essential tasks and considerations before launching your small business. Take your time to review each item and check them off as you complete them.

1. **Legal and Administrative Tasks:**

   - ☐ Register your business entity and obtain necessary licenses and permits.
   - ☐ Secure your business name and domain.
   - ☐ Set up your business bank account and obtain necessary insurance coverage.
   - ☐ Complete any required tax registrations and filings.

2. **Brand and Marketing:**

   - ☐ Finalize your brand identity, including your logo, colors, and brand messaging.
   - ☐ Develop a marketing plan and strategy for your launch, including social media, email marketing, and promotional activities.
   - ☐ Create marketing collateral such as website content, social media posts, and promotional materials.
   - ☐ Ensure your website is live and optimized for search engines.

3. **Product/Service Readiness:**

    ☐ Ensure your product/service is fully developed, tested, and ready for launch.
    ☐ Set pricing and packaging for your offerings.
    ☐ Create product/service documentation or instructions for customers, if applicable.

4. **Operations and Infrastructure:**

    ☐ Set up your physical location or office space, if applicable.
    ☐ Establish inventory management systems and procure necessary supplies or equipment.
    ☐ Implement technology systems and tools to support your operations and customer service.

5. **Team and Training:**

    ☐ Hire and train your team members, ensuring they are prepared for the launch.
    ☐ Communicate roles, responsibilities, and expectations to your team members.
    ☐ Conduct any necessary team meetings or training sessions to align everyone with the launch plan.

6. **Launch Planning and Execution:**

    ☐ Develop a detailed launch timeline with key milestones and deadlines.
    ☐ Execute your marketing strategy and promotional activities according to the timeline.
    ☐ Monitor the progress of your launch plan and make adjustments as needed.

7. **Customer Experience and Support:**

    - [ ] Prepare to provide excellent customer service and support to new customers.
    - [ ] Set up channels for customer inquiries, feedback, and support requests.
    - [ ] Train your team members on how to handle customer inquiries and resolve issues effectively.

8. **Post-Launch Evaluation:**

    - [ ] Plan to evaluate the success of your launch and gather feedback from customers.
    - [ ] Analyze key metrics and performance indicators to assess the effectiveness of your launch strategy.
    - [ ] Identify areas for improvement and make adjustments to your business strategy as needed.

Congratulations once again on reaching this exciting milestone in your entrepreneurial journey! By completing this checklist and launching your small business with careful planning and execution, you are setting yourself up for success in the competitive marketplace.

Promote Your Business

Chapter 17 - Craft Your Branding Strategy

Chapter 17

Craft Your Branding Strategy

Key Takeaways

- Defining Brand Identity and Values
- Creating Brand Messaging and Visuals
- Activity: Branding Strategy Workbook

Welcome to Chapter 17 of 'How to Start Your Own Kennel'! In this chapter, we will delve into the importance of crafting a strong branding strategy for your kennel business. Your brand is the heart and soul of your business, representing who you are, what you stand for, and how you differentiate yourself from competitors. As a small business owner, establishing a unique and compelling brand is crucial for attracting customers, building loyalty, and standing out in a crowded market.

Branding is more than just a logo or a catchy slogan, it is the overall perception that people have of your business. It encompasses everything from your visual identity to your tone of voice, from your customer experience to your values and mission. A well-defined brand not only helps you connect with your target audience but also builds trust and credibility in the minds of consumers.

As you embark on crafting your branding strategy, it's important to remember that consistency is key. Your brand should be reflected in every aspect of your business, from your website and social media presence to your packaging and customer interactions. By maintaining a cohesive and authentic brand image across all touchpoints, you will create a memorable and impactful experience for your customers.

In this chapter, we will guide you through the process of defining your brand identity and values, creating a compelling brand messaging, and developing visuals that resonate with your target audience. We will explore how to differentiate your brand from competitors, communicate your unique selling proposition, and establish a strong emotional connection with customers.

Whether you are just starting out or looking to refresh your existing brand, this chapter will provide you with the tools and insights you need to develop a successful branding strategy. By investing time and effort into crafting a strong brand, you will not only attract more customers but also build a loyal following that advocates for your business.

So, get ready to roll up your sleeves and dive into the exciting world of branding! Let's unleash the power of your brand and set your kennel business apart from the pack. Are you ready to make a lasting impression and leave a paw print in the hearts of your customers? Let's start crafting your branding strategy today!

Chapter 17 - Craft Your Branding Strategy

Defining Brand Identity and Values

Defining your brand identity and values is a crucial step in creating a strong and memorable brand for your kennel business. Your brand identity is how you want your business to be perceived by your customers, while your brand values are the principles and beliefs that guide your business decisions and actions. By clearly defining your brand identity and values, you can differentiate your business from competitors, build customer loyalty, and attract the right audience for your kennel.

Brand Identity:

Your brand identity encompasses the visual elements, messaging, and personality of your kennel business. It is what sets you apart from other kennels and helps customers recognize and remember your brand. When defining your brand identity, consider the following elements:

- **Logo:** Your logo is a visual representation of your brand and should be unique, memorable, and reflective of your kennel's personality. Consider hiring a professional designer to create a logo that aligns with your brand identity.

- **Color Palette:** Choose a color palette that conveys the emotions and feelings you want associated with your kennel. For example, earth tones like greens and browns can evoke a sense of nature and tranquility.

- **Typography:** Select fonts that are easy to read and complement your brand's personality. Whether you choose a modern sans-serif font or a classic serif font, consistency is key in establishing a cohesive brand identity.

- **Imagery:** Use high-quality images that showcase your kennel's facilities, services, and happy pets. Images should align with your brand values and resonate with your target audience.

- **Voice and Tone:** Define the tone of voice you want to use in your communication with customers. Whether you want to be friendly and approachable or professional and informative, consistency in tone helps build brand recognition.

Brand Values:

Your brand values are the guiding principles that shape your business culture, decision-making, and customer interactions. They communicate what your kennel stands for and what you believe in. When defining your brand values, consider the following aspects:

- **Pet Care Excellence:** Emphasize your commitment to providing top-quality care for pets in your kennel. This could include offering personalized services, maintaining a clean and safe environment, and hiring experienced staff.

- **Customer Service:** Prioritize exceptional customer service by listening to customer feedback, addressing concerns promptly, and going above and beyond to exceed customer expectations.

- **Community Involvement:** Demonstrate your kennel's dedication to giving back to the community through partnerships with local animal shelters, pet adoption events, or educational programs.

- **Sustainability:** Show your commitment to environmental sustainability by implementing eco-friendly practices in your kennel, such as using biodegradable cleaning products or reducing waste.

- **Transparency:** Build trust with your customers by being transparent about your kennel's policies, pricing, and services. Honesty and openness can help foster long-lasting relationships with pet owners.

Chapter 17 - Craft Your Branding Strategy

By defining your brand identity and values, you can create a cohesive and authentic brand that resonates with your target audience and sets your kennel apart in a competitive market. Remember to consistently communicate your brand identity and values across all touchpoints, from your website and social media profiles to your staff interactions and marketing materials. Your brand is a reflection of your business's values and mission, so take the time to define it thoughtfully and strategically.

Creating Brand Messaging and Visuals

Creating brand messaging and visuals is a crucial step in establishing a strong and memorable brand identity for your kennel business. Your brand messaging should convey your unique value proposition, mission, and personality, while your visuals should reflect your brand's aesthetics and evoke the right emotions in your target audience.

Brand Messaging:

- ***Define Your Unique Selling Proposition (USP):*** Identify what sets your kennel apart from competitors. Is it your personalized care for each pet, your state-of-the-art facilities, or your experienced staff? Your USP should be the foundation of your brand messaging.

- ***Create a Brand Voice:*** Determine the tone and language style that best represents your brand. Are you friendly and approachable, professional and knowledgeable, or fun and playful? Consistency in your brand voice across all communications is key.

- ***Craft Your Brand Story:*** Share the history, values, and passion behind your kennel in a compelling narrative. Your brand story should resonate with your target audience and create an emotional connection with them.

- ***Develop Key Messages:*** Identify the key points you want to communicate about your kennel, such as your commitment to pet safety, your expertise in animal care, or your dedication to customer satisfaction. These messages should be clear, concise, and impactful.

Chapter 17 - Craft Your Branding Strategy

Visual Branding:

- **Create a Logo:** Design a logo that visually represents your kennel's brand identity. Your logo should be simple, memorable, and versatile, as it will be used on various marketing materials, signage, and online platforms.

- **Select Brand Colors:** Choose a color palette that reflects the personality and values of your kennel. Consider the psychological effects of different colors, for example, blue conveys trust and professionalism, while green symbolizes health and nature.

- **Choose Brand Fonts:** Select fonts that are easy to read and align with your brand's voice and style. Use no more than two to three fonts consistently across all branding materials to maintain visual cohesion.

- **Design Brand Collateral:** Develop branded materials such as business cards, brochures, signage, and uniforms that showcase your logo, colors, and fonts. Consistent branding across all touchpoints reinforces brand recognition and credibility.

Remember, your brand messaging and visuals should resonate with your target audience and differentiate your kennel from competitors. Regularly review and refine your brand elements to ensure they remain relevant and appealing to your customers. By creating a strong and cohesive brand identity, you can build trust, loyalty, and recognition for your kennel business.

Chapter 17 - Craft Your Branding Strategy

> Visit **www.BusinessBookstore.com/start** to download blank forms, etc.

Activity: Branding Strategy Workbook

The Branding Strategy Workbook will guide you through the process of defining your brand identity, crafting compelling messaging, and designing visual elements that reflect your brand's essence. By completing this workbook, you'll create a roadmap for building a strong and cohesive brand that resonates with your audience.

Instructions:

1. **Brand Identity:**

   - Define your brand's vision, mission, and values.

     _____
     _____
     _____

   - Describe your brand personality and tone of voice.

     _____
     _____
     _____

   - Identify key attributes that differentiate your brand from competitors.

     _____
     _____
     _____

2. **Brand Messaging:**

- Craft your brand story, including its origins and aspirations.

  _____
  _____
  _____

- Define your value proposition and key messaging points.

  _____
  _____
  _____

- Develop taglines, slogans, or key phrases that encapsulate your brand essence.

  _____
  _____
  _____

3. **Visual Elements:**

☐ Design your logo, considering color, typography, and iconography.

☐ Choose a color palette and typography that align with your brand personality.

☐ Select imagery and visual style that reinforce your brand identity and messaging.

Chapter 17 - Craft Your Branding Strategy

4. **Consistency and Guidelines:**

☐ Design your logo, considering color, typography, and iconography.

☐ Choose a color palette and typography that align with your brand personality.

☐ Select imagery and visual style that reinforce your brand identity and messaging.

Brand Strategy Workbook Checklist:

☐ Define brand vision, mission, and values.

☐ Describe brand personality and tone of voice.

☐ Identify key brand attributes and differentiation factors.

☐ Craft brand story and value proposition.

☐ Develop taglines or key messaging points.

☐ Design logo and visual elements.

☐ Choose color palette and typography.

☐ Select imagery and visual style.

☐ Create brand guidelines for consistency.

☐ Review and refine branding strategy.

Conclusion:

Completing the Branding Strategy Workbook is a significant step towards building a strong and memorable brand for your business. Once you've filled out each section, you'll have a comprehensive blueprint that guides your brand's development and ensures consistency in messaging and visual representation. Let's unleash the full potential of your brand and make a lasting impression on your audience!

Chapter 18

Design Your Marketing Strategy

> **Key Takeaways**
>
> - Defining Target Markets and Objectives
> - Developing Marketing Mix
> - Activity: Marketing Plan Template

When it comes to defining your target markets and objectives for your kennel business, it's important to have a clear understanding of who your ideal customers are and what you want to achieve with your marketing efforts. By identifying your target markets and setting specific objectives, you can tailor your marketing strategies to reach the right audience and achieve your business goals.

Identifying Target Markets:

Start by conducting market research to identify the demographics, psychographics, and behaviors of your target audience. This will help you understand who your potential customers are, where they are located, and what they are looking for in a kennel service. Consider factors such as age, income level, lifestyle, and pet ownership status when defining your target markets.

For example, if your kennel offers luxury boarding services for high-income pet owners, your target market may include affluent individuals who value premium amenities and personalized care for their pets. On the other hand, if your kennel focuses on affordable daycare options for busy working professionals, your target market may consist of young professionals who need a reliable and convenient pet care solution.

Setting Objectives:

Once you have identified your target markets, it's important to set specific objectives that align with your business goals. Your objectives should be measurable, achievable, and relevant to your target audience. Consider what you want to accomplish with your marketing efforts, whether it's increasing brand awareness, attracting new customers, or boosting sales.

For example, if one of your target markets is pet owners in a specific neighborhood, your objective may be to increase brand awareness among local residents by distributing flyers and hosting community events. If another target market is pet parents who are active on social media, your objective may be to engage with them through targeted social media campaigns and influencer partnerships.

Chapter 18 - Design Your Marketing Strategy

Examples of Objectives:

- Increase brand awareness among target markets by 20% within six months.

- Generate 100 new leads from target markets through online advertising campaigns.

- Convert 50% of leads into paying customers through promotional offers and referral programs.

- Grow sales revenue from target markets by 15% year-over-year through upselling and cross-selling strategies.

Key Considerations:

When defining your target markets and objectives, keep in mind that your marketing strategies should be tailored to meet the specific needs and preferences of each audience segment. Consider factors such as communication channels, messaging tone, and promotional offers that resonate with your target markets.

Regularly review and adjust your target markets and objectives based on market trends, customer feedback, and business performance. By staying flexible and responsive to changing market dynamics, you can ensure that your kennel business remains competitive and relevant in the pet care industry.

Developing Marketing Mix

Developing a marketing mix is a crucial step in creating a successful marketing strategy for your kennel business. The marketing mix, also known as the 4Ps, consists of Product, Price, Place, and Promotion. By carefully considering each element of the marketing mix, you can effectively reach your target audience and drive sales.

- **Product:** The first element of the marketing mix is the product or service that you are offering. In the case of your kennel business, your primary product is pet boarding and grooming services. It is important to clearly define what sets your kennel apart from competitors. Consider offering unique services such as personalized grooming packages or specialized care for elderly pets to differentiate your business.

- **Price:** Pricing plays a significant role in attracting customers to your kennel. Research the pricing strategies of your competitors and determine a pricing structure that is competitive yet profitable for your business. Consider offering discounts for long-term boarding or bundled services to incentivize repeat business.

- **Place:** The place element of the marketing mix refers to the location and distribution channels of your kennel. Ensure that your kennel is conveniently located and easily accessible to your target audience. Consider partnering with local pet stores or veterinarians to promote your services and reach a wider customer base.

- **Promotion:** Promotion involves the marketing and advertising strategies used to promote your kennel business. Develop a comprehensive promotional plan that includes both online and offline marketing tactics. Utilize social media platforms to showcase your services and engage with potential customers. Consider running promotions such as referral discounts or seasonal specials to attract new clients.

It is important to remember that the elements of the marketing mix are interconnected and should work together to create a cohesive marketing strategy. Regularly evaluate and adjust your marketing mix based on customer feedback and market trends to ensure the continued success of your kennel business.

Example: Consider offering a loyalty program for frequent customers, where they earn points for each visit that can be redeemed for free services or discounts. This can help build customer loyalty and encourage repeat business.

Suggestion: Collaborate with local pet influencers or bloggers to promote your kennel services to a wider audience. Consider hosting a pet-friendly event or partnering with a pet rescue organization to raise awareness for your business.

> Visit **www.BusinessBookstore.com/start** to download blank forms, etc.

Activity: Marketing Plan Template

As you embark on developing your marketing plan, use the following template to organize your thoughts, strategies, and action steps. This template will guide you through key components of your marketing plan, ensuring that you address essential aspects of your marketing strategy.

1. **Executive Summary:**

   - Brief overview of your business and its marketing goals.
   - Summary of key strategies and tactics outlined in the marketing plan.

2. **Business Overview:**

   - Description of your business, its mission, and target market.
   - Analysis of your business's strengths, weaknesses, opportunities, and threats (SWOT).

3. **Market Analysis:**

   - Overview of the industry and market trends.
   - Analysis of target market demographics, psychographics, and buying behavior.
   - Assessment of competitors and their strategies.

4. **Marketing Objectives:**

   - Clear and measurable objectives aligned with overall business goals.
   - Specific targets for increasing brand awareness, acquiring customers, generating leads, etc.

5. **Marketing Strategy:**

    - Product positioning and differentiation strategy.
    - Pricing strategy and value proposition.
    - Distribution channels and logistics.
    - Promotional mix, including advertising, public relations, sales promotions, and digital marketing.

6. **Marketing Tactics:**

    - Detailed action plans for implementing marketing strategies.
    - Specific tactics for each element of the marketing mix.
    - Timeline for execution and deadlines for key milestones.

7. **Budget Allocation:**

    - Allocation of financial resources to different marketing activities.
    - Breakdown of costs for advertising, promotions, events, etc.

8. **Implementation Plan:**

    - Assignment of responsibilities to team members or external partners.
    - Schedule for executing marketing activities.
    - Monitoring and evaluation process to track progress and make adjustments as needed.

9. **Measurement and Analytics:**

    - Key performance indicators (KPIs) to measure the effectiveness of marketing efforts.
    - Tools and methods for tracking and analyzing performance data.
    - Plans for reporting and reviewing results regularly.

10. **Contingency Plan:**

    - Anticipated challenges or risks and strategies to mitigate them.
    - Backup plans in case of unforeseen circumstances affecting marketing activities.

Instructions:

1. Review each section of the marketing plan template carefully.

2. Fill in the relevant details and information based on your business's unique characteristics, goals, and market environment.

3. Ensure consistency and coherence across all sections to maintain a cohesive marketing strategy.

4. Regularly revisit and update your marketing plan as needed to adapt to changes in the market or business environment.

By completing this Marketing Plan Template, you'll have a comprehensive roadmap to guide your marketing efforts effectively and achieve your business objectives.

Chapter 19

Establish Your Online Presence

> **Key Takeaways**
> - Building a Professional Website
> - Creating Engaging Social Media Profiles
> - Activity: Website Checklist

> Visit **www.BusinessHelpStore.com** to search for your business domain.

Welcome to Chapter 19 of 'How to Start Your Own Kennel'! In this chapter, we will discuss the importance of establishing a strong online presence for your kennel business. In today's digital age, having a robust online presence is crucial for attracting customers, building brand awareness, and driving sales. Whether you are just starting out or looking to enhance your existing online presence, this chapter will provide you with the essential steps and strategies to succeed in the online world.

Promote Your Business

As a small business owner, creating a professional website and engaging social media profiles can help you connect with your target audience, showcase your services, and stand out from the competition. In this chapter, we will guide you through the process of building a website, creating social media content, and utilizing online marketing tools to reach your business goals.

Establishing your online presence is not just about having a website or social media accounts. It's about creating a digital footprint that reflects your brand identity, values, and unique selling points. By effectively leveraging online platforms, you can reach a wider audience, drive traffic to your physical location, and generate leads that convert into loyal customers.

Whether you are a tech-savvy entrepreneur or a beginner in the digital space, this chapter will provide you with practical tips, best practices, and actionable strategies to establish and enhance your online presence. From designing a user-friendly website to crafting compelling social media content, you will learn how to create a cohesive online strategy that resonates with your target market and drives business growth.

By the end of this chapter, you will have the knowledge and tools to confidently navigate the online landscape, engage with your audience, and build a strong online presence that sets your kennel business up for success. So, roll up your sleeves, get ready to dive into the world of online marketing, and take your kennel business to new heights!

Remember, in today's digital world, your online presence is often the first impression that potential customers have of your business. Make it count, make it memorable, and make it a true reflection of the passion and dedication you have for your kennel business. Let's get started on establishing your online presence and making a lasting impact in the digital realm!

Chapter 19 - Establish Your Online Presence

Building a Professional Website

Building a professional website for your kennel business is essential in today's digital age. Your website is often the first impression potential customers will have of your business, so it's important to make it visually appealing, easy to navigate, and informative. Here are some key steps to consider when creating your website:

1. **Choose a Domain Name:** Your domain name is your online address, so it should be easy to remember and relevant to your business. Consider using your kennel's name or a variation of it.

2. **Select a Website Builder:** There are many website builders available that make it easy to create a professional-looking website without the need for coding. Popular options include Wix, Squarespace, and WordPress.

3. **Design Your Layout:** Your website should have a clean and organized layout that showcases your services, pricing, and contact information. Consider using a simple color scheme that matches your branding.

4. **Create Engaging Content:** Use high-quality images of your kennel facilities, staff, and happy dogs to showcase your business. Write clear and concise copy that highlights your unique selling points and services.

5. **Include Contact Information:** Make it easy for potential customers to get in touch with you by including a contact form, phone number, and address on your website. Consider adding a map to show your location.

6. **Optimize for Search Engines:** Use relevant keywords throughout your website content to improve your search engine ranking. Consider creating a blog to regularly publish content related to dog care and training.

7. **Mobile-Friendly Design:** Ensure that your website is responsive and looks good on all devices, including smartphones and tablets. Many website builders offer mobile optimization features.

8. **Include Testimonials:** Showcase positive reviews and testimonials from satisfied customers to build trust with potential clients. Consider adding a dedicated page for testimonials or featuring them on your homepage.

9. **Integrate Social Media:** Link your website to your social media profiles to encourage visitors to follow you on platforms like Facebook, Instagram, and Twitter/X. Consider adding social media sharing buttons to your content.

10. **Regularly Update Your Content:** Keep your website fresh and engaging by regularly updating your content, adding new photos, and posting blog articles. This will show visitors that your business is active and up-to-date.

By following these steps and paying attention to detail, you can create a professional website that effectively promotes your kennel business and attracts new customers. Remember to regularly monitor your website's performance and make adjustments as needed to ensure it continues to meet your business goals.

Chapter 19 - Establish Your Online Presence

Creating Engaging Social Media Profiles

Social media is a powerful tool for marketing your kennel business and engaging with your audience. Creating engaging social media profiles is essential to attract followers, increase brand awareness, and drive traffic to your website. Here are some tips to help you create compelling social media profiles:

1. **Choose the Right Platforms:** Before creating your social media profiles, research which platforms your target audience uses the most. Popular platforms for businesses include Facebook, Instagram, Twitter/X, and LinkedIn. Each platform has its own unique features and audience demographics, so choose the ones that align with your business goals.

2. **Complete Your Profile:** Make sure to fill out all the necessary information in your social media profiles. This includes your business name, logo, bio, contact information, and website link. A complete profile builds credibility and makes it easier for potential customers to learn more about your kennel.

3. **Use High-Quality Visuals:** Visual content is key to grabbing the attention of social media users. Use high-quality images and videos that showcase your kennel facilities, services, and happy dogs. Consider hiring a professional photographer to capture stunning visuals for your profiles.

4. **Write Compelling Copy:** Your social media bio and posts should be engaging and informative. Use a friendly tone that resonates with your audience and clearly communicates your unique selling points. Highlight what sets your kennel apart from competitors and why pet owners should choose your services.

5. **Post Consistently:** Consistency is key to maintaining an active social media presence. Create a content calendar to plan out your posts in advance and ensure a regular posting schedule. This keeps your audience engaged and informed about upcoming events, promotions, and news related to your kennel.

6. **Interact with Your Audience:** Social media is a two-way communication channel. Respond to comments, messages, and mentions promptly to show that you value your followers' feedback. Engage with your audience by asking questions, running polls, and sharing user-generated content to foster a sense of community.

7. **Utilize Hashtags:** Hashtags help increase the visibility of your social media posts and reach a wider audience. Research relevant hashtags in the pet care industry and include them in your posts to attract users who are interested in dog-related content. Create a branded hashtag for your kennel to encourage user-generated content and build brand awareness.

8. **Promote User Reviews and Testimonials:** Encourage satisfied customers to leave reviews and testimonials on your social media profiles. Positive feedback from happy pet owners can build trust and credibility for your kennel. Share these reviews on your profiles to showcase the quality of your services and attract new customers.

9. **Monitor Analytics:** Track the performance of your social media profiles using analytics tools provided by each platform. Monitor key metrics such as engagement rate, reach, and follower growth to assess the effectiveness of your social media strategy. Use this data to refine your content and optimize your profiles for better results.

Chapter 19 - Establish Your Online Presence

By following these tips and strategies, you can create engaging social media profiles that attract followers, drive traffic to your website, and boost brand awareness for your kennel business. Remember to stay authentic, consistent, and responsive to build a strong online presence and connect with your target audience effectively.

Chapter 19 - Establish Your Online Presence

Activity: Website Checklist

Before launching your website, it's important to ensure that it meets certain standards and includes essential elements to provide a positive user experience and effectively showcase your brand. Use the following checklist to review your website and make any necessary adjustments:

> Visit **www.BusinessHelpStore.com** to search for your business domain.

1. **Domain Name:**

   ☐ Domain name is relevant to your business.

   ☐ Domain name is easy to spell and remember.

   ☐ Domain is registered and active.

2. **Hosting:**

   ☐ Website is hosted on a reliable server.

   ☐ Hosting plan provides adequate bandwidth and storage.

3. **Design and Layout:**

   ☐ Website design is visually appealing and consistent with your brand identity.
   ☐ Layout is user-friendly and easy to navigate.

   ☐ Mobile responsiveness: Website is optimized for mobile devices and displays properly on various screen sizes.

4. **Content:**

   ☐ All content is clear, concise, and error-free.

   ☐ Contact information (phone number, email address, physical address) is prominently displayed.

   ☐ About Us page provides information about your business, mission, and values.

   ☐ Product or service pages include detailed descriptions, pricing, and images.

   ☐ Testimonials or customer reviews are showcased to build credibility.

5. **Navigation:**

   ☐ Navigation menu is easy to find and navigate.

   ☐ Website has a logical hierarchy with clearly defined categories and subcategories.

   ☐ Internal links are used to guide users to relevant pages within the website.

6. **SEO Optimization:**

   ☐ Meta titles and descriptions are optimized with relevant keywords.

   ☐ Image alt text is used to describe images for improved accessibility and SEO.

   ☐ Website content is optimized for search engines to improve visibility and rankings.

Chapter 19 - Establish Your Online Presence

7. **Security:**

    ☐ Website has an SSL certificate installed to encrypt data and secure online transactions.
    ☐ Backup system is in place to protect against data loss or website downtime.

8. **Functionality:**

    ☐ Forms (contact forms, signup forms, etc.) are functional and submit data correctly.
    ☐ Links and buttons are working properly and lead to the intended destinations.
    ☐ E-commerce functionality (if applicable) is fully operational, including shopping cart, checkout process, and payment gateway integration.

9. **Legal Compliance:**

    ☐ Privacy policy is in place and accessible to users.

    ☐ Terms and conditions are provided for website visitors.

    ☐ Website complies with relevant laws and regulations, such as GDPR or CCPA (if applicable).

10. **Analytics and Tracking:**

    ☐ Website analytics tool (such as Google Analytics) is installed to track website traffic, user behavior, and other key metrics.
    ☐ Conversion tracking is set up to monitor the performance of marketing campaigns and goals.

Once you have completed the items on this checklist and made any necessary adjustments, your website will be ready to launch and effectively represent your business online.

Chapter 20

Implement Social Media Marketing

> **Key Takeaways**
>
> - Choosing Social Media Platforms
> - Creating Content and Engagement Strategies
> - Activity: Social Media Strategy Planner

Welcome to Chapter 20 of 'How to Start Your Own Kennel'! In today's digital age, social media has become an essential tool for businesses of all sizes to connect with their audience, build brand awareness, and drive sales. As a small business owner, leveraging social media marketing can help you reach a wider audience, engage with your customers, and ultimately grow your business.

With the rise of social media platforms such as Facebook, Instagram, Twitter/X, and LinkedIn, businesses now have the opportunity to connect with potential customers on a more personal level. By creating compelling content, engaging with your audience, and utilizing targeted advertising, you can effectively promote your kennel and attract new customers.

However, implementing a successful social media marketing strategy requires careful planning, consistent effort, and a deep understanding of your target audience. In this chapter, we will guide you through the process of developing and executing a social media marketing plan that aligns with your business goals and resonates with your customers.

Whether you are new to social media marketing or looking to enhance your existing strategy, this chapter will provide you with practical tips, best practices, and actionable steps to help you make the most of your social media presence. From choosing the right platforms to creating engaging content to measuring your success, we will cover everything you need to know to succeed in the world of social media marketing.

By the end of this chapter, you will have the knowledge and tools to effectively leverage social media to promote your kennel, engage with your audience, and drive business growth. So, roll up your sleeves, get ready to dive into the world of social media marketing, and take your kennel to new heights!

Chapter 20 - Implement Social Media Marketing

Choosing Social Media Platforms

When it comes to choosing social media platforms for your kennel business, it's important to consider where your target audience spends their time online. Different platforms have different demographics and features, so selecting the right ones can help you reach and engage with your customers effectively.

Here are some popular social media platforms to consider:

- **Facebook:** With over 2 billion active users, Facebook is a great platform for reaching a wide audience. You can create a business page, share updates, photos, and videos, and interact with your followers through comments and messages.

- **Instagram:** If visual content is a key part of your marketing strategy, Instagram is a must. You can share photos and videos of your kennel, pets, and events, and use hashtags to reach a larger audience.

- **Twitter/X:** Twitter/X is known for its real-time updates and conversations. You can share short updates, news, and engage with your followers through tweets and replies.

- **Pinterest:** Pinterest is a visual discovery platform where users can find and save ideas. If you offer pet grooming or DIY pet projects, Pinterest can be a great platform to showcase your work and drive traffic to your website.

- **LinkedIn:** If you offer professional services or want to connect with other businesses, LinkedIn is a great platform for networking and establishing your expertise in the industry.

When choosing social media platforms, consider the following factors:

- **Target Audience:** Where does your target audience spend their time online? Choose platforms that align with their demographics and interests.

- **Content Type:** What type of content do you plan to share? Choose platforms that support the format you want to use, whether it's photos, videos, or text-based posts.

- **Engagement Level:** How do you plan to engage with your audience? Some platforms are better suited for real-time interactions, while others are more focused on visual content or professional networking.

- **Resources:** Consider the time and resources you have available to manage your social media presence. It's better to have a strong presence on a few platforms than to spread yourself too thin across multiple platforms.

It's important to have a presence on multiple platforms to reach a wider audience, but focus on quality over quantity. Choose platforms that align with your business goals and where you can consistently create and share engaging content.

Remember to monitor your social media performance regularly and adjust your strategy based on what works best for your kennel business. Each platform has its own analytics tools to track your performance and engagement metrics, so use them to optimize your social media efforts.

Chapter 20 - Implement Social Media Marketing

Creating Content and Engagement Strategies

Creating content and engagement strategies is essential for attracting and retaining customers for your kennel business. By providing valuable and engaging content, you can build a strong relationship with your audience and increase brand awareness. Here are some tips to help you create effective content and engagement strategies:

1. **Understand Your Audience:** Before creating any content, it's important to understand your target audience. Consider their demographics, interests, and preferences. This will help you tailor your content to meet their needs and engage them effectively.

2. **Define Your Objectives:** Determine what you want to achieve with your content and engagement strategies. Whether it's increasing brand awareness, driving website traffic, or generating leads, having clear objectives will guide your content creation process.

3. **Create Valuable Content:** Provide content that is informative, entertaining, and relevant to your audience. This could include blog posts, videos, infographics, or social media posts. Make sure your content adds value to your audience and helps solve their problems.

4. **Consistent Brand Messaging:** Maintain a consistent brand voice and messaging across all your content channels. This will help build brand recognition and trust with your audience. Ensure that your content reflects your brand values and personality.

5. **Engage with Your Audience:** Encourage two-way communication with your audience by responding to comments, messages, and feedback. Engaging with your audience shows that you value their input and helps build a loyal community around your brand.

6. **Use Visuals:** Incorporate visuals such as images, videos, and infographics into your content. Visuals are more engaging and can help convey your message more effectively. Make sure your visuals are high-quality and relevant to your content.

7. **Optimize for SEO:** Ensure that your content is optimized for search engines by including relevant keywords, meta descriptions, and alt tags. This will help improve your visibility in search engine results and attract more organic traffic to your website.

8. **Share Customer Stories:** Share testimonials, success stories, and customer reviews to showcase the positive experiences of your customers. This social proof can help build trust with potential customers and encourage them to engage with your brand.

9. **Collaborate with Influencers:** Partner with influencers or industry experts to create content that reaches a wider audience. Influencers can help amplify your message and increase brand awareness among their followers.

10. **Monitor and Analyze Performance:** Track the performance of your content and engagement strategies using analytics tools. Monitor key metrics such as website traffic, engagement rates, and conversion rates. Use this data to refine your strategies and optimize your content for better results.

By implementing these strategies, you can create compelling content that resonates with your audience and drives engagement for your kennel business. Remember to stay consistent, experiment with different types of content, and always prioritize providing value to your audience.

Chapter 20 - Implement Social Media Marketing

Visit **www.BusinessBookstore.com/start** to download blank forms, etc.

Activity: Social Media Strategy Planner

Congratulations on reaching the stage where you're ready to craft a comprehensive social media strategy for your business! This activity will guide you through the process of developing a strategic plan to effectively leverage social media platforms for your business objectives.

Instructions:

1. **Define Your Goals:** Start by clearly outlining your social media goals. What do you aim to achieve through your social media efforts? Examples include increasing brand awareness, driving website traffic, generating leads, fostering customer engagement, and boosting sales.

2. **Identify Your Target Audience:** Describe your target audience in detail, including demographics, interests, behaviors, and pain points. Understanding your audience will help you tailor your content and messaging to resonate with them effectively.

3. **Choose Social Media Platforms:** Select the social media platforms that align with your target audience and business goals. Consider factors such as platform demographics, user engagement, and content format preferences.

4. **Content Strategy:** Outline the key elements of your content strategy, including content themes, types, frequency, and tone of voice. Determine the topics you'll cover, the formats you'll use, and the posting schedule you'll follow.

© 2024 BusinessBookstore.com

5. **Engagement Tactics:** Identify strategies to encourage audience engagement and interaction on social media. This may include asking questions, running polls or contests, responding to comments, and sharing user-generated content.

6. **Content Calendar:** Create a content calendar outlining the timing and frequency of your social media posts. This calendar will help you stay organized, plan ahead, and maintain consistency in your posting schedule.

7. **Monitoring and Analysis:** Establish metrics to measure the success of your social media efforts. Track key performance indicators (KPIs) such as reach, engagement, clicks, conversions, and ROI. Regularly analyze your data to identify trends, insights, and areas for improvement.

8. **Adjustment and Optimization:** Based on your analysis, make adjustments to your social media strategy as needed. Experiment with different tactics, content formats, and posting times to optimize your results and achieve your goals more effectively.

Social Media Strategy Planner:

1. **Goals:**

   _____

   _____

   _____

2. **Target Audience:**

   _____

   _____

   _____

Chapter 20 - Implement Social Media Marketing

3. **Social Media Platforms:**

   _____

   _____

   _____

4. **Content Strategy:**
   - Content Themes: _____
   - Content Types: _____
   - Posting Frequency: _____
   - Tone of Voice: _____

5. **Engagement Tactics:**

   _____

   _____

   _____

6. **Content Calendar:**

   _____

   _____

   _____

7. **Monitoring and Analysis:**

   _____

   _____

   _____

8. **Adjustment and Optimization:**

_____

_____

_____

By completing this Social Media Strategy Planner, you'll have a clear roadmap for implementing your social media strategy and achieving your business objectives. Remember to regularly review and update your strategy to stay aligned with your evolving business goals and audience preferences.

Chapter 20 - Implement Social Media Marketing

Date	Platform	Content type	Content Description	Focused Keywords	KPI
Ex. 1/1/24	Facebook	Video	Google my business guide	Google My Business Help	Likes and Views

Chapter 21

Create Content for Your Business

> **Key Takeaways**
> - Content Planning and Ideation
> - Content Creation and Distribution
> - Activity: Content Calendar

Welcome to Chapter 21 of 'How to Start Your Own Kennel'! In this chapter, we will discuss the importance of creating content for your business and how it can help you attract and engage customers. As a small business owner, it is crucial to have a solid content strategy in place to showcase your products or services, establish your expertise in the industry, and build relationships with your target audience.

Content creation is a powerful tool that can help you differentiate your business from competitors, drive traffic to your website, and ultimately increase sales. Whether you are writing blog posts, creating videos, or designing infographics, the content you produce should be informative, engaging, and relevant to your target market.

In this chapter, we will guide you through the process of planning, creating, and distributing content for your business. We will cover topics such as content planning and ideation, content creation best practices, and how to develop a content calendar to ensure consistency in your messaging.

By the end of this chapter, you will have a clear understanding of how to leverage content marketing to grow your business and connect with your customers on a deeper level. So, grab a pen and notebook, and let's get started on creating compelling content that will set your kennel apart in the market!

Remember, content is king in today's digital age, and by investing time and effort into developing high-quality content, you can position your business as a trusted authority in the industry and attract a loyal following of customers who value what you have to offer. So, let's roll up our sleeves and dive into the exciting world of content creation!

Chapter 21 - Create Content for Your Business

Content Planning and Ideation

Content planning and ideation are crucial aspects of creating engaging and valuable content for your kennel business. By strategically planning your content and generating creative ideas, you can attract and retain customers, build brand awareness, and drive sales. In this section, we will explore the steps involved in content planning and ideation to help you develop a successful content strategy for your kennel business.

1. **Understand Your Audience:** The first step in content planning is to understand your target audience. By knowing who your customers are, their preferences, interests, and pain points, you can create content that resonates with them. Consider creating customer personas to have a clear picture of your audience demographics, behaviors, and needs.

2. **Set Clear Goals:** Before creating content, it's essential to define your goals. Whether you aim to increase brand awareness, drive website traffic, generate leads, or boost sales, having clear objectives will guide your content strategy. Make sure your goals are specific, measurable, achievable, relevant, and time-bound (SMART).

3. **Brainstorm Content Ideas:** Once you have a good understanding of your audience and goals, it's time to brainstorm content ideas. Consider the type of content that will resonate with your audience, such as blog posts, videos, infographics, social media posts, or newsletters. Think about topics that are relevant to your kennel business, such as pet care tips, training advice, customer testimonials, or behind-the-scenes stories.

4. **Use Content Calendar:** Creating a content calendar can help you organize and plan your content effectively. A content calendar allows you to schedule when and where your content will be published, ensuring a consistent and cohesive content strategy. Consider using tools like Google Calendar, Trello, or CoSchedule to manage your content calendar.

5. **Focus on Quality Over Quantity:** While it's essential to publish regular content, quality should always be a top priority. Focus on creating valuable, informative, and engaging content that provides value to your audience. Avoid creating content just for the sake of publishing and instead, strive to deliver content that educates, entertains, or inspires your audience.

6. **Repurpose Content:** Don't be afraid to repurpose your existing content to reach a broader audience and maximize its impact. For example, you can turn a blog post into a video, create an infographic from a case study, or compile customer testimonials into a social media post. Repurposing content can save time and resources while extending the lifespan of your content.

7. **Stay Consistent:** Consistency is key to building a strong online presence and engaging your audience. Whether it's posting on social media, sending newsletters, or updating your blog, maintaining a consistent publishing schedule will help you stay top-of-mind with your customers. Consider setting a content cadence that works for your business and sticking to it.

8. **Track and Measure Results:** Lastly, it's essential to track and measure the performance of your content to see what's working and what's not. Use analytics tools like Google Analytics, social media insights, or email marketing metrics to monitor key performance indicators (KPIs) such as website traffic, engagement rates, conversion rates, and ROI. Use this data to optimize your content strategy and make informed decisions moving forward.

Chapter 21 - Create Content for Your Business

By following these content planning and ideation strategies, you can create compelling content that resonates with your audience, drives engagement, and ultimately helps you achieve your business goals. Remember to stay creative, adaptive, and customer-focused in your content creation process to stand out in the competitive kennel industry.

Content Creation and Distribution

Content creation and distribution are essential components of any successful marketing strategy. In today's digital age, creating high-quality, engaging content is crucial for attracting and retaining customers. In this section, we will explore the importance of content creation, different types of content you can create, and how to effectively distribute your content to reach your target audience.

Why is content creation important?

Content creation plays a vital role in building brand awareness, establishing credibility, and driving customer engagement. By consistently producing valuable and relevant content, you can position yourself as an industry expert and connect with your audience on a deeper level. Additionally, well-crafted content can help improve your website's search engine ranking and attract organic traffic.

Types of content to create:

- **Blog posts:** Writing informative and engaging blog posts can help showcase your expertise and provide valuable information to your audience. Consider topics that are relevant to your industry and address common questions or pain points your customers may have.

- **Infographics:** Visual content like infographics can be a powerful way to convey complex information in a visually appealing format. Use tools like Canva or Piktochart to create eye-catching infographics that are easy to share on social media.

- **Video content:** Videos are becoming increasingly popular on social media platforms. Consider creating how-to videos, product demonstrations, or behind-the-scenes footage to engage your audience and showcase your brand personality.

Chapter 21 - Create Content for Your Business

- **Case studies:** Sharing success stories and customer testimonials can help build trust with potential customers. Highlighting real-life examples of how your products or services have benefited others can be a compelling way to convince prospects to choose your business.

Effective content distribution strategies:

1. **Social media:** Utilize social media platforms like Facebook, Instagram, Twitter/X, and LinkedIn to share your content with a wider audience. Tailor your content to each platform's unique features and engage with your followers through likes, comments, and shares.

2. **Email marketing:** Build an email list of subscribers who are interested in receiving updates from your business. Send out regular newsletters with links to your latest blog posts, videos, or promotions to keep your audience engaged and informed.

3. **Guest blogging:** Collaborate with industry influencers or other businesses to write guest blog posts for their websites. This can help you reach a new audience and establish credibility in your field.

4. **SEO:** Optimize your content for search engines by using relevant keywords, meta tags, and high-quality backlinks. This can help improve your website's visibility in search engine results and drive organic traffic to your site.

Remember, the key to successful content creation and distribution is consistency and quality. Regularly publishing valuable content that resonates with your target audience can help you build a loyal following and drive business growth. Experiment with different types of content and distribution channels to see what works best for your business, and don't be afraid to adjust your strategy based on feedback and analytics.

Chapter 21 - Create Content for Your Business

> Visit **www.BusinessBookstore.com/start** to download blank forms, etc.

Activity: Content Calendar

Creating a content calendar is a strategic way to plan and organize your content initiatives across various channels. This tool allows you to map out your content strategy, schedule publication dates, and ensure consistency in your messaging. Follow the steps below to create your own content calendar:

1. **Identify Content Themes and Topics:** Start by brainstorming content ideas that align with your business objectives and resonate with your target audience. Consider seasonal trends, industry events, and customer pain points when selecting topics for your content calendar.

2. **Outline Content Formats and Channels:** Determine the types of content you'll create, such as blog posts, videos, infographics, or social media posts. Choose the channels where you'll distribute each piece of content, such as your website, blog, social media platforms, or email newsletters.

3. **Assign Publication Dates:** Use a calendar template to assign publication dates to each piece of content. Consider factors such as content frequency, publishing cadence, and seasonal trends when scheduling your content. Be realistic about your bandwidth and resources when setting publication dates.

4. **Allocate Resources and Responsibilities:** Identify team members or external collaborators responsible for creating, editing, and publishing each piece of content. Clearly define roles and responsibilities to ensure smooth execution and accountability throughout the content creation process.

5. **Incorporate SEO Keywords and Optimization:** Integrate relevant keywords and SEO optimization techniques into your content calendar to enhance the discoverability and search visibility of your content. Align your content topics with keyword research and SEO best practices to attract organic traffic to your website.

6. **Include Promotion and Distribution Strategies:** Plan how you'll promote and distribute your content across various channels to maximize its reach and impact. Incorporate social media promotion, email marketing, paid advertising, and content syndication into your content calendar to amplify your message.

7. **Monitor and Analyze Performance:** Regularly monitor the performance of your content initiatives using analytics tools and metrics such as website traffic, engagement rates, social media metrics, and conversion metrics. Use data-driven insights to optimize your content strategy and refine your content calendar over time.

Conclusion:

By creating a comprehensive content calendar, you can streamline your content planning process, maintain consistency in your messaging, and optimize the effectiveness of your content initiatives. Use the provided template to organize your content strategy and keep track of your content schedule. Remember to adapt and iterate your content calendar based on evolving business needs, audience feedback, and performance insights.

Chapter 21 - Create Content for Your Business

Date	Content Topic	Content Format	Distribution Channel	Responsible Party

Chapter 22 - Plan Advertising and Promotions

Chapter 22

Plan Advertising and Promotions

> **Key Takeaways**
>
> - Budgeting for Advertising Campaigns
> - Selecting Advertising Channels and Methods
> - Activity: Advertising Campaign Planner

Welcome to Chapter 22 of 'How to Start Your Own Kennel'! As a small business owner, one of the most crucial aspects of your success is your ability to effectively promote your products or services to your target audience. In this chapter, we will delve into the world of advertising and promotions, exploring different strategies and methods that can help you attract new customers and grow your business.

Advertising and promotions play a significant role in creating awareness about your kennel, generating interest in your services, and ultimately driving sales. Whether you are just starting out or looking to expand your existing business, having a solid advertising and promotions plan in place is essential for reaching your business goals.

Throughout this chapter, we will discuss the importance of budgeting for advertising campaigns, selecting the right advertising channels and methods, and creating compelling promotional materials that resonate with your target audience. By the end of this chapter, you will have a clear understanding of how to develop a comprehensive advertising and promotions strategy that aligns with your business objectives.

As a small business owner, it's important to remember that advertising and promotions are not one-size-fits-all. What works for one business may not necessarily work for another. It's essential to tailor your advertising and promotions strategy to your specific business needs, target audience, and budget constraints.

Whether you choose to invest in traditional advertising methods such as print ads, radio commercials, or direct mail campaigns, or opt for digital marketing strategies like social media advertising, email marketing, or search engine optimization, the key is to be strategic and intentional in your approach. By carefully planning and executing your advertising and promotions efforts, you can maximize your return on investment and achieve long-term success for your kennel.

Throughout this chapter, we will provide you with practical tips, tools, and resources to help you navigate the complex world of advertising and promotions. From setting advertising budgets and analyzing the effectiveness of your campaigns to refining your messaging and targeting the right audience, we will cover all the essential steps to help you create a successful advertising and promotions plan.

Remember, advertising and promotions are not just about selling your products or services, they are about building relationships with your customers, establishing your brand identity, and creating a lasting impression in the minds of your target audience. By approaching advertising and promotions with a strategic mindset and a customer-centric focus, you can set your kennel up for long-term growth and success.

Chapter 22 - Plan Advertising and Promotions

So, are you ready to take your advertising and promotions efforts to the next level? Let's dive in and explore the exciting world of promoting your kennel to the world!

Budgeting for Advertising Campaigns

Budgeting for advertising campaigns is a crucial aspect of your marketing strategy. Allocating the right amount of money to promote your kennel can help you reach your target audience effectively and generate more leads and sales. Here are some key steps to consider when budgeting for advertising campaigns:

1. **Set Clear Goals:** Before you start budgeting for advertising, it's essential to define your advertising goals. Are you looking to increase brand awareness, drive website traffic, or boost sales? Having clear objectives will help you determine how much you need to spend on advertising.

2. **Calculate Your Total Budget:** Determine how much money you can allocate towards advertising. Consider factors such as your overall marketing budget, revenue goals, and the cost of other business expenses. It's recommended to spend around 5-10% of your total revenue on advertising, depending on your industry and business size.

3. **Identify Your Target Audience:** Understanding your target audience is crucial when budgeting for advertising. Different demographics and customer segments may require different advertising strategies and channels. Consider conducting market research to identify the most effective ways to reach your target audience.

4. **Choose the Right Advertising Channels:** There are various advertising channels available, including online (social media, search engine marketing, display ads) and offline (print, radio, TV). Select the channels that align with your target audience and advertising goals. For example, if you're targeting a younger audience, investing in social media advertising may be more effective.

Chapter 22 - Plan Advertising and Promotions

5. **Estimate Costs:** Research the costs associated with different advertising channels. Some channels, like social media advertising, allow you to set a specific budget based on your goals (e.g., cost per click or cost per impression). Other channels, such as print or TV ads, may require a fixed budget based on the placement and duration of the ad.

6. **Allocate Budget Wisely:** Once you have estimated the costs for each advertising channel, allocate your budget accordingly. Consider investing more in channels that have a higher return on investment (ROI) or those that have been successful in reaching your target audience in the past.

7. **Track and Measure Results:** Monitoring the performance of your advertising campaigns is essential to determine their effectiveness. Use tools like Google Analytics or social media insights to track key metrics such as website traffic, conversions, and engagement. Analyzing these metrics will help you optimize your advertising budget for future campaigns.

Remember, budgeting for advertising campaigns is an ongoing process. It's essential to regularly review and adjust your advertising budget based on the performance of your campaigns and changes in your business goals. By following these steps and investing wisely in advertising, you can effectively promote your kennel and attract more customers.

Selecting Advertising Channels and Methods

When it comes to advertising your kennel business, selecting the right channels and methods is crucial to reaching your target audience effectively. By choosing the most appropriate advertising platforms, you can maximize your marketing efforts and attract potential customers. Here are some key considerations to keep in mind when selecting advertising channels and methods:

1. **Understand Your Target Audience:** Before deciding on advertising channels, it's essential to have a clear understanding of your target audience. Consider factors such as demographics, interests, and behavior to determine where your potential customers are most likely to be reached.

2. **Choose Relevant Channels:** Based on your target audience analysis, select advertising channels that are most likely to resonate with your potential customers. For example, if your target audience spends a significant amount of time on social media, investing in social media advertising may be a wise choice.

3. **Consider Your Budget:** Determine how much you are willing to invest in advertising and choose channels that align with your budget. Some advertising platforms may be more cost-effective than others, so make sure to evaluate the potential return on investment for each channel.

4. **Evaluate Channel Effectiveness:** Monitor the performance of each advertising channel to assess its effectiveness in reaching your target audience and driving results. Use analytics tools to track key metrics such as click-through rates, conversion rates, and return on ad spend.

Chapter 22 - Plan Advertising and Promotions

5. **Test Different Methods:** Experiment with different advertising methods to see which ones yield the best results for your kennel business. Consider running A/B tests to compare the performance of different ad creatives, messaging, and targeting strategies.

6. **Utilize a Mix of Channels:** Instead of relying on a single advertising channel, consider using a mix of channels to reach a wider audience and increase brand visibility. Combining online and offline advertising methods can help you reach customers through multiple touchpoints.

7. **Stay Consistent:** Consistency is key in advertising, so make sure to maintain a regular presence on chosen channels to keep your brand top of mind for potential customers. Develop a content calendar to plan out your advertising campaigns and ensure a steady flow of messaging.

8. **Seek Professional Help:** If you're unsure about which advertising channels and methods are best for your kennel business, consider seeking advice from marketing professionals or agencies. They can provide valuable insights and expertise to help you make informed decisions.

Example:

For example, if your target audience consists of pet owners in a specific geographic area, you may consider advertising in local newspapers, pet magazines, and community newsletters. Additionally, running targeted Facebook ads or Google AdWords campaigns can help you reach pet owners who are actively searching for kennel services online.

Conclusion:

By carefully selecting advertising channels and methods that align with your target audience and business goals, you can effectively promote your kennel business and attract new customers. Regularly evaluate the performance of your advertising efforts and make adjustments as needed to optimize your marketing strategy for success.

Chapter 22 - Plan Advertising and Promotions

> Visit **www.BusinessBookstore.com/start** to download blank forms, etc.

Activity: Content Calendar

Creating a content calendar is a strategic way to plan and organize your content initiatives across various channels. This tool allows you to map out your content strategy, schedule publication dates, and ensure consistency in your messaging. Follow the steps below to create your own content calendar:

1. **Identify Content Themes and Topics:** Start by brainstorming content ideas that align with your business objectives and resonate with your target audience. Consider seasonal trends, industry events, and customer pain points when selecting topics for your content calendar.

2. **Outline Content Formats and Channels:** Determine the types of content you'll create, such as blog posts, videos, infographics, or social media posts. Choose the channels where you'll distribute each piece of content, such as your website, blog, social media platforms, or email newsletters.

3. **Assign Publication Dates:** Use a calendar template to assign publication dates to each piece of content. Consider factors such as content frequency, publishing cadence, and seasonal trends when scheduling your content. Be realistic about your bandwidth and resources when setting publication dates.

4. **Allocate Resources and Responsibilities:** Identify team members or external collaborators responsible for creating, editing, and publishing each piece of content. Clearly define roles and responsibilities to ensure smooth execution and accountability throughout the content creation process.

5. **Incorporate SEO Keywords and Optimization:** Integrate relevant keywords and SEO optimization techniques into your content calendar to enhance the discoverability and search visibility of your content. Align your content topics with keyword research and SEO best practices to attract organic traffic to your website.

6. **Include Promotion and Distribution Strategies:** Plan how you'll promote and distribute your content across various channels to maximize its reach and impact. Incorporate social media promotion, email marketing, paid advertising, and content syndication into your content calendar to amplify your message.

7. **Monitor and Analyze Performance:** Regularly monitor the performance of your content initiatives using analytics tools and metrics such as website traffic, engagement rates, social media metrics, and conversion metrics. Use data-driven insights to optimize your content strategy and refine your content calendar over time.

Content Calendar Template:

Date	Content Topic	Content Format	Distribution Channel	Responsible Party

Conclusion:

By creating a comprehensive content calendar, you can streamline your content planning process, maintain consistency in your messaging, and optimize the effectiveness of your content initiatives. Use the provided template to organize your content strategy and keep track of your content schedule. Remember to adapt and iterate your content calendar based on evolving business needs, audience feedback, and performance insights.

Chapter 23

Manage Customer Relationships

> **Key Takeaways**
>
> - Implementing Customer Relationship Management Systems
> - Providing Excellent Customer Service
> - Activity: CRM Implementation Checklist

Welcome to Chapter 23 of 'How to Start Your Own Kennel'! As a small business owner, managing customer relationships is crucial to the success and growth of your kennel. Building strong connections with your customers can lead to repeat business, positive word-of-mouth referrals, and ultimately, increased revenue.

In this chapter, we will explore the importance of implementing customer relationship management systems and providing excellent customer service. By focusing on these areas, you can ensure that your customers feel valued, appreciated, and satisfied with their experience at your kennel.

Customer relationship management (CRM) is more than just a software system, it is a strategy that allows you to track, analyze, and improve interactions with your customers. By implementing CRM systems, you can gain valuable insights into customer preferences, behavior, and feedback. This information can help you tailor your services to better meet the needs and expectations of your customers.

Providing excellent customer service is another key component of managing customer relationships. By delivering exceptional service, you can build trust, loyalty, and long-lasting relationships with your customers. Whether it's responding promptly to inquiries, resolving issues quickly and effectively, or going above and beyond to exceed customer expectations, every interaction with a customer is an opportunity to strengthen your relationship.

In the following sections, we will discuss how to implement CRM systems effectively, provide tips for delivering exceptional customer service, and offer practical strategies for managing customer relationships. By following the advice and recommendations in this chapter, you can create a positive and memorable experience for your customers, leading to increased satisfaction and loyalty.

Remember, happy customers are loyal customers. By prioritizing customer relationships and focusing on providing outstanding service, you can set your kennel apart from the competition and build a strong and loyal customer base. Your customers are the lifeblood of your business, so it's essential to invest time and effort into nurturing those relationships.

So let's dive into Chapter 23 and learn how to effectively manage customer relationships for the success and growth of your kennel. By implementing the strategies and techniques outlined in this chapter, you can create a customer-centric business that thrives on positive relationships and satisfied customers. Let's get started!

Chapter 23 - Manage Customer Relationships

Implementing Customer Relationship Management Systems

Customer Relationship Management (CRM) systems are essential tools for managing and nurturing relationships with your customers. These systems help businesses track customer interactions, manage sales pipelines, and improve overall customer satisfaction. Here are some key steps to consider when implementing a CRM system for your kennel business:

1. **Evaluate Your Business Needs:** Before selecting a CRM system, assess your business requirements and goals. Determine what features are essential for your kennel business, such as contact management, lead tracking, and reporting capabilities.

2. **Research CRM Options:** There are various CRM systems available in the market, each offering different features and pricing plans. Research different CRM providers, read reviews, and compare their offerings to find the best fit for your business.

3. **Customize Your CRM:** Once you have selected a CRM system, customize it to align with your kennel business processes. Set up custom fields, workflows, and automation rules to streamline your customer management tasks.

4. **Train Your Team:** Provide training to your team members on how to use the CRM system effectively. Ensure they understand how to input customer data, track interactions, and generate reports to improve customer relationships.

5. **Integrate Your CRM:** Integrate your CRM system with other business tools and platforms, such as your website, email marketing software, and social media channels. This will help centralize customer data and streamline communication channels.

6. **Track Customer Interactions:** Use your CRM system to record and track all customer interactions, including phone calls, emails, and in-person visits. This data will provide valuable insights into customer preferences and behaviors.

7. **Segment Your Customer Base:** Segment your customer base based on factors such as purchase history, preferences, and demographics. This will allow you to tailor your marketing messages and services to meet the specific needs of each customer segment.

8. **Personalize Customer Communications:** Leverage your CRM system to send personalized messages and offers to your customers. Use customer data to create targeted marketing campaigns that resonate with their interests and preferences.

By implementing a CRM system in your kennel business, you can effectively manage customer relationships, improve customer satisfaction, and drive business growth. Remember to regularly update and maintain your CRM system to ensure it continues to meet the evolving needs of your business and customers.

Chapter 23 - Manage Customer Relationships

Providing Excellent Customer Service

Providing excellent customer service is crucial for the success of your kennel business. Happy customers are more likely to become repeat clients and recommend your services to others. Here are some key tips to help you deliver exceptional customer service:

1. **Listen to Your Customers:** One of the most important aspects of providing excellent customer service is listening to your customers. Take the time to understand their needs, concerns, and feedback. This will show them that you value their opinions and are committed to providing the best possible service.

2. **Be Responsive:** Make sure to respond to customer inquiries, questions, and concerns in a timely manner. Whether it's through phone, email, or social media, being responsive shows that you care about your customers and their needs.

3. **Go the Extra Mile:** Sometimes, providing excellent customer service means going above and beyond what is expected. This could be anything from offering a personalized service to providing a small gift or discount for their loyalty.

4. **Train Your Staff:** Your employees play a crucial role in delivering great customer service. Make sure to provide them with the necessary training and resources to handle customer inquiries and concerns effectively.

5. **Ask for Feedback:** Encourage your customers to provide feedback on their experience with your kennel. This will not only help you improve your services but also show customers that their opinions are valued.

Here are some specific examples of how you can provide excellent customer service in your kennel business:

- **Personalized Greeting:** When customers arrive at your kennel, greet them by name and ask about their pet. This personal touch will make them feel valued and appreciated.

- **Follow-Up Calls:** After a customer picks up their pet, follow up with a phone call to ensure everything went well. This shows that you care about their satisfaction and are committed to providing a positive experience.

- **Customer Loyalty Program:** Implement a loyalty program that rewards customers for their repeat business. This could be in the form of discounts, free services, or exclusive perks.

- **Quick Resolution of Issues:** If a customer has a complaint or concern, address it promptly and find a solution that satisfies them. This will show that you take customer feedback seriously and are willing to make things right.

- **Thank You Notes:** Send thank you notes or emails to customers after they use your services. Express your gratitude for their business and invite them to return in the future.

Chapter 23 - Manage Customer Relationships

> Visit **www.BusinessBookstore.com/start** for a list of CRM systems.

Activity: CRM Implementation Checklist

Congratulations on taking the step to implement a Customer Relationship Management (CRM) system for your small business! This checklist will guide you through the process of setting up and implementing your CRM system effectively. Before you begin, ensure that you have selected a CRM platform that aligns with your business needs and goals.

Instructions:

- ☐ Review each item on the checklist carefully.

- ☐ Check off each task as you complete it.

- ☐ Customize the checklist according to your specific CRM implementation plan and requirements.

CRM Implementation Checklist:

1. **Define Objectives:**

   - ☐ Clearly define the objectives and goals you aim to achieve with the CRM implementation.
   - ☐ Identify key performance indicators (KPIs) to measure the success of your CRM initiative.

2. **Select CRM Platform:**

    ☐ Choose a CRM platform that meets your business requirements, budget, and scalability needs.
    ☐ Ensure the CRM platform integrates seamlessly with your existing systems and software.

3. **Data Migration:**

    ☐ Evaluate existing customer data and determine the scope of data migration.
    ☐ Cleanse and organize customer data to ensure accuracy and completeness.
    ☐ Develop a data migration plan and schedule to transfer data to the new CRM system.

4. **Customization and Configuration:**

    ☐ Customize the CRM system to align with your business processes and workflows.
    ☐ Configure user permissions and access levels based on roles within your organization.

5. **Training and Onboarding:**

    ☐ Provide comprehensive training to users on how to use the CRM system effectively.
    ☐ Develop training materials, such as user guides and tutorials, to support user onboarding.
    ☐ Schedule regular training sessions and refresher courses to ensure ongoing user proficiency.

Chapter 23 - Manage Customer Relationships

6. **Integration with Other Systems:**

    ☐ Integrate the CRM system with other business-critical systems, such as accounting software, email marketing platforms, and e-commerce platforms.
    ☐ Test integrations to ensure data flows seamlessly between systems without errors.

7. **Data Security and Compliance:**

    ☐ Implement robust data security measures to protect sensitive customer information.
    ☐ Ensure compliance with relevant data protection regulations, such as GDPR or CCPA.

8. **User Adoption and Feedback:**

    ☐ Encourage user adoption by soliciting feedback from users and addressing any concerns or challenges they encounter.
    ☐ Regularly review CRM usage metrics and user feedback to identify areas for improvement.

9. **Continuous Improvement:**

    ☐ Establish a process for ongoing system maintenance, updates, and enhancements.
    ☐ Regularly review and refine CRM configurations and workflows to optimize efficiency and effectiveness.

By completing this CRM implementation checklist, you are taking significant steps toward leveraging technology to enhance your customer relationships and drive business growth. Be diligent in your implementation efforts, and don't hesitate to seek assistance from CRM experts or consultants if needed.

Chapter 24

Develop Your Sales Strategy

> **Key Takeaways**
> - Setting Sales Targets and Goals
> - Creating Sales Processes and Pipelines
> - Activity: Sales Funnel Analysis

Welcome to Chapter 24 of 'How to Start Your Own Kennel'! In this chapter, we will be discussing how to develop an effective sales strategy for your kennel business. Sales are the lifeblood of any business, and having a well-thought-out sales strategy is crucial to driving revenue and growth.

As a small business owner, it can be daunting to think about selling your products or services. However, developing a sales strategy doesn't have to be intimidating. By understanding your target market, setting clear sales goals, and implementing proven sales techniques, you can create a successful sales strategy that will help your kennel business thrive.

In this chapter, we will guide you through the process of developing a sales strategy that aligns with your business goals and objectives. We will explore how to set realistic sales targets, create effective sales processes, and build a strong sales pipeline to drive consistent revenue for your kennel business.

Whether you are a seasoned entrepreneur or just starting out, this chapter will provide you with the tools and insights you need to develop a sales strategy that works for your kennel business. By focusing on understanding your customers' needs, providing exceptional customer service, and implementing proven sales techniques, you can increase your sales and grow your business.

Throughout this chapter, we will provide you with practical tips, actionable advice, and real-world examples to help you develop a sales strategy that sets your kennel business up for success. By following the steps outlined in this chapter and putting in the effort to implement them effectively, you can take your sales to the next level and achieve your business goals.

Remember, developing a sales strategy is an ongoing process that requires dedication, persistence, and a willingness to learn from both successes and failures. By continuously refining and optimizing your sales strategy based on feedback and results, you can ensure that your kennel business remains competitive and profitable in the long run.

So, are you ready to take your sales strategy to the next level? Let's dive in and explore how you can develop a sales strategy that drives revenue, builds customer relationships, and sets your kennel business up for long-term success. Get ready to unleash your sales potential and watch your business grow!

Chapter 24 - Develop Your Sales Strategy

Setting Sales Targets and Goals

Setting sales targets and goals is a crucial step in ensuring the success of your kennel business. By establishing clear objectives for your sales team, you can motivate them to perform at their best and drive revenue growth. In this section, we will discuss the importance of setting sales targets and goals, as well as provide some tips on how to do so effectively.

Why Set Sales Targets and Goals?

Setting sales targets and goals helps to provide focus and direction for your sales team. It gives them something concrete to work towards and enables you to measure their performance against specific benchmarks. By setting targets, you can also track progress, identify areas for improvement, and make adjustments to your sales strategy as needed.

How to Set Sales Targets and Goals

When setting sales targets and goals, it is important to make them SMART: Specific, Measurable, Achievable, Relevant, and Time-bound.

1. **Specific:** Clearly define what you want to achieve. For example, increase monthly sales by 20%.

2. **Measurable:** Ensure that your goals can be quantified so that you can track progress. Use metrics such as revenue, number of sales, or customer acquisition rate.

3. **Achievable:** Set realistic targets that are within reach based on your current resources and market conditions.

4. **Relevant:** Align your sales targets with your overall business objectives. For example, if your goal is to expand your customer base, your sales targets should focus on acquiring new customers.

5. **Time-bound:** Establish a deadline for achieving your sales targets. This creates a sense of urgency and helps to keep your team motivated.

Example:

Let's say your kennel business aims to increase revenue by 15% in the next quarter. Your sales target could be to generate $10,000 in new sales each month for the next three months. This target is specific, measurable, achievable, relevant, and time-bound.

Additional Tips for Setting Sales Targets and Goals:

- ***Involve Your Sales Team:*** Get input from your sales team when setting targets. This will help to ensure buy-in and commitment to achieving the goals.

- ***Break Down Targets:*** Divide larger goals into smaller, manageable targets. This can help to prevent overwhelm and keep your team motivated.

- ***Monitor Progress:*** Regularly track and review your sales targets to assess performance. Celebrate successes and make adjustments as needed to stay on track.

- ***Provide Incentives:*** Consider offering rewards or bonuses for achieving or exceeding sales targets. This can help to boost motivation and drive performance.

By setting clear and achievable sales targets and goals, you can empower your sales team to drive revenue growth and contribute to the success of your kennel business.

Chapter 24 - Develop Your Sales Strategy

Creating Sales Processes and Pipelines

Creating sales processes and pipelines is essential for the success of your kennel business. A well-defined sales strategy will help you attract new customers, retain existing ones, and ultimately grow your revenue. In this section, we will discuss the key steps to developing effective sales processes and pipelines for your kennel.

1. **Define Your Sales Process:** Start by outlining the steps that a potential customer will go through from the initial contact to making a purchase. This may include lead generation, qualification, presentation, negotiation, and closing. By clearly defining your sales process, you can ensure that all team members are on the same page and working towards the same goal.

2. **Identify Your Target Audience:** Understand who your ideal customers are and tailor your sales process to meet their needs. For example, if your target audience is pet owners who value convenience, you may want to focus on highlighting your kennel's convenient location, flexible hours, and online booking system during the sales process.

3. **Establish Sales Goals and Targets:** Set specific, measurable sales goals to track your progress and motivate your team. For example, you may aim to increase sales by 20% in the next quarter or acquire 50 new customers by the end of the year. Break down these goals into smaller targets for individual team members to ensure accountability.

4. **Develop a Sales Pipeline:** A sales pipeline is a visual representation of the stages that a prospect goes through during the sales process. This can help you track the progress of each lead, identify bottlenecks, and prioritize your efforts. Consider using a CRM system to manage your sales pipeline effectively.

5. **Implement Sales Automation Tools:** Utilize sales automation tools to streamline your sales processes and improve efficiency. For example, you can use email marketing software to send personalized follow-up emails to leads, or a customer relationship management (CRM) system to track customer interactions and manage sales opportunities.

6. **Train Your Sales Team:** Provide your sales team with the necessary training and resources to effectively execute the sales process. This may include product knowledge training, sales techniques, objection handling, and customer service skills. Regular coaching and feedback can help improve performance and drive results.

7. **Monitor and Analyze Sales Performance:** Regularly review your sales metrics and KPIs to assess the effectiveness of your sales processes. Identify areas of improvement, celebrate successes, and make data-driven decisions to optimize your sales strategy. Consider holding weekly or monthly sales meetings to discuss performance and share best practices.

8. **Continuously Improve Your Sales Processes:** Seek feedback from customers, team members, and stakeholders to identify opportunities for improvement in your sales processes. Stay updated on industry trends, competitor strategies, and customer preferences to adapt your sales approach accordingly. Experiment with new techniques, technologies, and channels to stay ahead of the competition.

By following these steps and continuously refining your sales processes and pipelines, you can drive growth and success for your kennel business. Remember, sales is a dynamic and ever-evolving field, so stay agile, adaptable, and customer-focused to achieve your sales goals.

Chapter 24 - Develop Your Sales Strategy

> Visit **www.BusinessBookstore.com/start** to download blank forms, etc.

Activity: Sales Funnel Analysis

Instructions:

Performing a sales funnel analysis is crucial for understanding the effectiveness of your sales efforts and identifying areas for improvement. Use the checklist below to assess each stage of your sales funnel and identify opportunities to optimize your sales process.

Lead Generation:

- ☐ Evaluate lead generation channels (e.g., website, social media, email campaigns) for effectiveness.
- ☐ Determine the volume and quality of leads generated from each channel.
- ☐ Identify which lead sources are driving the highest conversion rates.

Lead Qualification:

- ☐ Review lead qualification criteria and scoring system.
- ☐ Assess the percentage of leads that meet qualification criteria.
- ☐ Identify common reasons for disqualification and adjust criteria if necessary.

Engagement and Nurturing:

☐ Analyze engagement metrics such as email open rates, click-through rates, and website interactions.
☐ Review the effectiveness of nurturing campaigns in moving leads through the sales funnel.
☐ Identify opportunities to improve lead engagement and increase conversion rates.

Sales Conversion:

☐ Evaluate the percentage of qualified leads that progress to the sales stage.
☐ Review sales conversion rates at each stage of the sales process.
☐ Identify potential barriers to conversion and strategies to overcome them.

Closing the Sale:

☐ Analyze the effectiveness of sales tactics and strategies in closing deals.
☐ Review the average sales cycle length and identify opportunities to shorten it.
☐ Assess the percentage of leads that convert into paying customers.

Chapter 24 - Develop Your Sales Strategy

Post-Sale Follow-Up:

☐ Evaluate customer retention efforts and strategies.

☐ Assess customer satisfaction and gather feedback on the sales experience.
☐ Identify opportunities to upsell or cross-sell additional products or services.

Overall Funnel Performance:

☐ Calculate overall conversion rates and sales funnel efficiency.

☐ Compare current performance metrics to historical data or industry benchmarks.
☐ Identify areas of strength and weakness in the sales funnel and develop action plans for improvement.

Conclusion:

By completing this sales funnel analysis, you'll gain valuable insights into the effectiveness of your sales process and uncover opportunities to optimize performance, increase conversions, and drive revenue growth.

Next Steps:

☐ Implement changes and improvements based on the findings of your analysis.
☐ Continuously monitor and track sales funnel metrics to measure the impact of your optimizations.
☐ Regularly revisit and refine your sales funnel analysis to ensure ongoing success and adaptation to changing market dynamics.

Chapter 25

Conclusion

> **Key Takeaways**
> - Glossary
> - Additional Resources
> - Franchises

Congratulations on reaching the end of this workbook on starting your own kennel! You've come a long way in planning and preparing for your new business venture. Remember, every successful business owner started with a dream and took small steps to turn that dream into reality.

As you move forward, stay focused on your goals, stay resilient in the face of challenges, and never lose sight of your passion for dogs and the joy they bring to people's lives. Running a kennel can be a rewarding and fulfilling experience, and with the right mindset and determination, you can make it a success.

Conclusion

If you ever feel overwhelmed or unsure of your next steps, remember that you are not alone. There are many resources available to support you on your journey, including business books on various topics for small business owners. I encourage you to visit BusinessBookstore.com to explore a wide range of helpful resources that can guide you in your entrepreneurial endeavors.

Best of luck in your kennel business, and may your passion for dogs continue to inspire you every step of the way!

Chapter 25 - Conclusion

What's Next?

Congratulations on completing this comprehensive guide on starting your own kennel! By now, you should have a solid foundation in place to launch your business successfully. But what's next?

Here are some key steps to consider as you move forward:

1. **Execute Your Launch Plan:** Now that you have your business plan in place, it's time to put it into action. Follow your launch timeline and marketing strategy to introduce your kennel to the world. Make sure to track your progress and adjust your tactics as needed.

2. **Monitor and Evaluate:** Once your kennel is up and running, it's crucial to monitor your performance and evaluate your results. Keep track of key metrics such as revenue, customer feedback, and marketing ROI. Use this data to make informed decisions and optimize your operations.

3. **Build Your Brand:** Continue to develop your branding strategy to strengthen your identity in the market. Consistent branding across all touchpoints will help you stand out and attract loyal customers. Consider investing in professional design services to enhance your visual assets.

4. **Expand Your Online Presence:** As digital marketing continues to grow, it's essential to maintain a strong online presence. Regularly update your website with fresh content, engage with your audience on social media, and explore new digital channels to reach potential customers.

5. **Nurture Customer Relationships:** Customer satisfaction is key to the success of your kennel. Focus on providing excellent service, personalized experiences, and ongoing communication with your clients. Implement a customer relationship management system to streamline your interactions and build long-term loyalty.

Conclusion

6. **Scale Your Business:** As your kennel grows, consider opportunities for expansion and diversification. Explore new services, locations, or partnerships to reach a broader audience and increase your revenue. Stay agile and adapt to market trends to stay ahead of the competition.

7. **Stay Informed:** Keep yourself updated on industry trends, regulations, and best practices in the pet care sector. Attend conferences, workshops, and networking events to connect with other professionals and learn from their experiences. Continuous learning is essential for long-term success.

Remember, starting your own kennel is a challenging but rewarding journey. Stay focused, remain resilient, and never stop striving for excellence. With dedication and hard work, you can build a thriving business that brings joy to both pets and their owners.

Best of luck on your entrepreneurial adventure!

APPENDIX

Glossary

- **Advertising Campaign:** A series of advertisements with a specific goal or message, typically run across multiple channels.

- **Brand Identity:** The visual and emotional representation of a brand, including logos, colors, and messaging.

- **Business Plan:** A document outlining the goals, strategies, and financial projections of a business.

- **Customer Relationship Management (CRM):** A system for managing interactions with customers, including tracking leads and customer service.

- **Franchise:** A business model in which an individual buys the rights to operate a business under a established brand.

- **Goal Setting:** The process of defining objectives and creating a plan to achieve them.

- **Market Research:** The process of gathering information about a target market to inform business decisions.

- **Startup Costs:** The expenses incurred when starting a new business, including equipment, marketing, and legal fees.

- **SWOT Analysis:** An evaluation of a business's strengths, weaknesses, opportunities, and threats.

- **Target Audience:** The specific group of people that a business aims to reach with its products or services.

© 2024 BusinessBookstore.com

Appendix

Additional Resources

- BusinessBookstore.com - www.businessbookstore.com
- American Kennel Club (AKC) - www.akc.org
- Pet Industry Association of America (PIAA) - www.piaa.net
- Small Business Administration (SBA) - www.sba.gov
- Entrepreneur.com - www.entrepreneur.com

These resources provide valuable information and tools to help you start and grow your own kennel business. Visit their websites for articles, guides, templates, and more to support you on your entrepreneurial journey.

Franchises

- **Dogtopia:** A leading dog daycare and boarding franchise with a focus on socialization and exercise for dogs.
  1-866-963-8489. www.dogtopia.com

- **Camp Bow Wow:** A premier doggy daycare and overnight camp franchise that offers a fun and safe environment for dogs to play and socialize.
  1-877-700-2275. www.campbowwow.com

- **Pet Paradise:** A luxury pet boarding, daycare, and grooming franchise that provides a resort-like experience for pets.
  1-866-965-5340. www.petparadise.com

- **PetSmart PetsHotel:** A pet boarding and daycare franchise that offers a variety of services for dogs and cats, including grooming and training.
  1-888-839-9638. www.petsmart.com/petshotel

- **Central Bark Doggy Day Care:** A dog daycare franchise that focuses on providing a safe and fun environment for dogs to play and socialize.
  1-866-799-2275. www.centralbarkusa.com

Appendix

Notes

Notes

Notes

Notes

Notes

Made in the USA
Middletown, DE
07 October 2024

62159677R00168